AN OUTLOOK ON
OUR
INNER
WESTERN
WAY

WILLIAM G. GRAY

SAMUEL WEISER   NEW YORK

First published by
Samuel Weiser, Inc.
740 Broadway
New York, N.Y. 10003

ISBN 0-87728-493-8

Typesetting and layout by
Positive Type
Millerton, N.Y. 12546

Printed in the U.S.A. by
Noble Offset Printers, Inc.
New York, N.Y. 10003

Contents

1. Our Western Inner Way

Considering the widespread revival of interest in the occult in recent years, it is still surpising how few people raised in the West are consciously aware of its unique Inner Tradition—the secret spirituality behind our Western way of life. It has not only made us what we are today, but, more importantly, it can help prepare us for the future. This reaches far deeper than our historical or cultural heritage alone. It is the lineage and progress of what can only be called the 'Western Soul', which develops as we evolve upon this planet.

This evolution is perceptible from a purely spiritual viewpoint, quite apart from the restricted beliefs and physical boundaries of material existence. Unless we strive to reach beyond rationality, and acquaint ourselves with the spiritual and magical realms where our 'Real Selves' reside, we shall never understand the purpose of our incarnation. To understand these inner spheres of reality, we must enter and *experience* them.

Perhaps the greatest single obstacle to achieving this awareness lies in the extraordinary elusiveness of our Western Inner Way. If we were seeking enlightenment through the mystical or spiritual disciplines of the Orient, we would have well-defined paths on every side. Yet, when we try to contact equivalent systems in the West, we discover an apparently disjointed collection of Folk tales and apocryphal writings, interpreted through the bigotry and ignorance of modern commentators and translators. At present, our surviving traditions, and their revivals and adaptations, would take entire incarnations to trace—let alone evaluate. In future generations, who knows what could—or will—be constructed out of something so superficially confusing and conflicting. It is fortunate for us that a few souls in each generation have the patience and dedication to find—and follow—this old line of faith in Life, which steadily leads toward the Western Way of Enlightenment. To discover this as individuals, we must plunge very deep, avoiding surface obstructions that hinder us from consciously claiming our rightful, but carefully concealed heritage.

*   *   *

What *is* the Inner Way of the West? Anyone asking this question in all sincerity will encounter strange replies from many unexpected quarters. Unfortunately, the intentions of many would-be guides to the Inner Planes are more like guided missiles aimed at the seeker's wallet. Seldom have so many sharks snapped so eagerly as the unsuspecting plunge into deep occult waters unsupported by anything except a well-inflated money belt. From mystic supply shops to witch covens, 'Orders' of this, that, and other, stretch greedy hands toward the gullible. None but the truly poor in spirit could possibly navigate through such pirate-infested waters and emerge enriched by the experience.

Incredibly, the muddle confronting modern pilgrims of the Western Way is actually part and parcel of its program. It can be considered a contemporary version of the dangerous and delusive 'Dweller on the Threshold' who guarded the gates of the ancient Mysteries. This fabled horror represents everything in ourselves that seeks to prevent us from achieving a state of spiritual perfection. Either we challenge and conquer this negative side of our nature, or we remain an outsider and get no closer, consciously, to the truth of our Inner Identities.

This is exactly the problem set before us by the reputed representatives of our 'Hidden Holy Tradition'. What, if anything, is genuine and what is deceptive? For those able to detect the difference, and make their way through the workings of the Western Mysteries, this is a crucial test. In the past, this quest was illustrated by the popular folktale of a hero striving for some lofty objective. The goal was usually to be found in a stronghold whose environs concealed every imaginable obstacle and trap—some coercive, others dangerous, and a few even fatal. Yet, none of them were insurmountable, providing the young hopeful used his resourcefulness, and obeyed instructions frequently imparted to him by an older and wiser well wisher. Eventually, guided by his own inspiration, and the possible assistance of a good fairy, he managed to overcome all obstacles and gain access to the goal itself. The point being, of course, that his maneuvering through these preparatory trials brought out the qualities of character essential to his ultimate success. Unless he had possessed the personal resources necessary to overcome the lesser difficulties, he would have been totally unfit to cope with more crucial ones.

All of this applies directly to our Western Inner Way. Its spiritual actuality is indeed surrounded by a vast field of misleading, inaccurate and diversionary material. We might well suppose that its appointed guardians have camouflaged its paths very cleverly against unworthy entrants and unwelcome intruders. Only those intelligent and determined enough to penetrate the barriers and surmount the formidable obstacles are likely to reach the realities symbolized by the goal. Through this filtering system, sometimes called the 'Outer Court', aspiring souls sort themselves out stage by stage as they respond to various spiritual stimuli. In this way, they select their own status and either make consistent progress toward truer systems of living, or remain stranded at some particular level until ready to release themselves and continue along a corrected course.

Therefore, from a spiritual viewpoint, all the apparent rubbish, absurdity and commercial claptrap obscuring the entrances to our Western Inner Tradition are really quite valuable. Nothing else categorizes seekers of genuine selfways to Illumination so quickly and effectively as this 'acid test' of occult acumen. Well-meaning meanderers through the Outer Court usually come to little harm apart from wasted time and money, and they may actually, eventually, produce some useful experiences. Over-eager enthusiasts frequently become happily absorbed with the toys and games left around for children to play with, and cheerfully pass a lifetime in amiable amusement. Those with more devious motivations frequently injure themselves with the very tools they pick up in hopes of hurting others. Only those few with the ability to find their way through the tangles of this thorny area step by step will come anywhere close to the truths.

As an example, it is obvious that none of the catchpenny claimants to modern occult supermarketry can possibly provide anything except expensive entertainment or overpriced handicrafts. Nothing of a purely spiritual nature can ever be purchased or bartered. Thus, any claims involving the sale of spiritual powers, privileges, or specific properties, are by their very nature false. However, for something to be false, there must, by necessity, be some truth proving it so. Once we realize how to read the directions correctly, whatever falsehoods have attached themselves to our Tradition will also act as indicators of its truths. In a sense, we might expect our Western Inner Way to contain a core of truth protected by a defensive covering of falsehood and deception. The more our Tradition is misused and mistreated, the thicker and more confusing that covering becomes. Just as the body produces scar tissue over a wound, an injury to the soul reacts much the same. Since a Tradition expresses the soul of a people, it follows similar laws. Our tradition has suffered a great deal of this scarring during its long life, and has consequently developed a protective layer over the entrances to the depths from whence it derives, and where the final decisions concerning our ultimate destiny are made. It is small wonder, then, that paths to the Inner Tradition of the West are so hard to find.

In a magical sense, actual membership in the Western Mysteries is a matter of birth and blood, and there are many souls entitled to that distinction who are not consciously aware of their potential. But, to become an active Companion of the Western Way, with an initiated intelligence, is quite a step. Qualifications for that degree of achievement can be extrememly demanding, and probationary periods are usually very long. Only the most devoted and dedicated souls are likely to exalt themselves enough to contact even the relatively minor levels of Inner life. Nevertheless, if one is brave enough to face the trials, no genuine applicant seeking admission to the Outer Court is ever denied a chance to claim his birthright. Even individuals who don't intend to deliberately pursue spiritual advancement in this incarnation would be well advised to make all possible inquiries about our Tradition. Knowledge is never wasted, and what we pour back into our common store of consciousness will always be available for future earth lives.

Let's begin by looking at the origins of the Western Way to see how—and why—it is different from the traditions of other parts of the world. To answer this clearly, we must start with the dawn of human differentiation, when mankind was slowly sorting itself into the distinct categories of consciousness needed for proper adaption to life at each level of existence. As primal inhabitants of this earth, we were steadily moving ourselves into suitable positions for collective and individual relationships, and, potential spiritual entities, we were slowly establishing our inner existence along parallel lines. This is to say, that we were establishing our existence in conformity with the cosmic pattern which originally produced us from what we have come to call 'the Void' or 'Nothing', since we can discern nothing at all of its true nature. The accepted symbol of our pattern of evolution is the Cosmic Cross, which describes this dynamic and indefinable Life in all its aspects.

First, imagine the early planetary sphere as a centrifuge, steadily impelling souls toward whichever level or condition corresponds best to their predominant characteristics. This produced four major variations, arranged according to the gravitational and magnetic fields of the earth itself. We can distinguish these divisions as follows:

1. EASTERN—against the direction of the spin.
2. WESTERN—with the direction of the spin.
3. EQUATORIAL—receiving the maximum effect of the spin.
4. POLAR—receiving the minimum effect of the spin.

Both recorded history and recent archeological investigations indicate that the first civilizations developed in the East. What trends, then, led mankind in divergent directions? Strictly speaking, motivation for such movement usually arose from a conflict of temperaments. The migratory instinct in man has always resulted in a movement away from an environment where attitudes have been at variance, in search of places and people who are more in sympathy with new aims and ideals. It is a basic story of attraction and repulsion. We live in a bi-polar world of alternating light and dark and tend to follow these principles wherever they apply. In this case, we began in the East with mankind massed together in close communities which grew into cities and nations. These communities were usually governed by an establishment of privileged persons exercising a central control through either military, economic or religious means. By and large, individualism sank beneath the sheer weight of collectivism and individual identity was submerged in a sea of imposed conventions and herd habits. Millions still accept this condition quite willingly and are content to remain subservient for many incarnations. Out of such general conditions grew the Tradition of the East.

At the other extreme, the divine destiny of man manifests as an inherent process of individuation into an immortal spiritual state. Those who heard this cosmic call, but were frustrated in its fulfilment by conditions of human society, were faced with one option—they must move in search of freedom. Thus, a westerly migration of such souls continued in a constant stream, taking with it whatever culture and customs were suitable to their new mission. But, however these traditions were employed, the increasing importance of the individual in the community became more accented as the generations passed. As collectivism overtook static settlements, migrations reached farther and farther west until finally, during the last centuries, the circle has closed—with the saturation point in America. So grew the Tradition of the West.

The Equatorial Tradition developed through those who, without great drives in any direction, merely sought to live in lush conditions of provident nature with a minimum of effort, and preferably without dictatorial interference. Theirs was the *dolce far niente* way of life. They were content to subsist unambitiously from day to day, while dreaming of glorious tomorrows full of miracles.

Opposing this is the Polar Tradition, which arose among those who felt the need of individuation so strongly that they were prepared to face the hardest and toughest conditions of this world in its pursuit. They wrung their lives out of remote and inhospitable regions out of a desire for independence. For them, adversity was something to be attacked and conquered. Action was their way out of anything, and isolation was a state of spirit to achieve with fierce pride.

Originally, this distribution of human temperament was largely geographical, but it has become more and more a matter of character alone as to which people are best suited to particular traditions. Since we are concerned with the rise and development of the Western Tradition in particular, it is highly important to recognize its roots in the human instinct of individuation. In other words, for a true Westerner, the community and its culture exists primarily to provide the individual with the background necessary to achieve his own aims. The improvement of individual status is of paramount importance, and the concept of 'State' is merely a mutual service intended to assist such an end. This may sound very idealistic, but it is the fundamental factor behind the entire Western Tradition—however far we fall short of it. Unless this point is entirely appreciated and understood, the Inner Way of our Tradition cannot possibly be recognized, far less followed or practiced with any degree of fidelity. The keynote of our Inner Western Tradition could be called 'mutual monadism'—people aiding each other to become individual members of the Supreme Spirit, acknowledged as the Ultimate Entity.

If we do not fully appreciate the roots of our Tradition, there is little hope of understanding how it grew and how its various branches of belief developed. Perhaps worse, it will not be seen that this tradition is *an actual living fact* which is our foundation and is drawing us into a future alive with the hope and confidence for this world or any other world we may reach.

Ask one person what comprises the Western Tradition and they would reply Druidism. Another would say Qabalism, and another Rosicrucianism, while others would put in claims for ancient fairy-faiths, Celtic gods, or supposed survivals of primitive paganism now miscalled "witchcraft." Some would certainly say Christianity. There is a wide choice, yet all that can be truly said of such systems is that they are just branches or offshoots of a Tradition existing as a purely spiritual structure in its own right, rooted in the absolute core of our being beyond the reach of ordinary human consciousness. This is what is so important to realize: There exists within us a fundamental "life faith", linking past, present, and future in a Tradition to which we belong because we live in its "spiritual stream". We can no more escape or evade this reality than we might expect to stay alive without eating, or breathing. What matters most is how these Traditions are translated into spiritual systems which mankind can pursue on the different life-levels in order to become more evolved creatures of consciousness.

As difficult as it may be, we have to see our true Inner Tradition as a specific spiritual storehouse out of which we interpret ideas in whatever ways we suppose or believe will help us in the general direction of our drift towards a state of perfection which could perhaps be called Divinity. As we work our way along, the summations of our experiences—or experiments—are incorporated into the Tradition as additives or modifications. This is, of course, entirely dependent on the extent to which we actually *live* the Tradition, rather than just existing round its edges.

From our deepest possible Life-drives come impulses which urge our conscious activites in a definite spiritual direction. These are not formalized at first, but consist of what we might consider "energized intentions". As this inner energy comes closer and closer to levels of ordinary human consciousness, it passes through processes which structure and focus it into concepts and ideas we can comprehend as people living in this world. According to the nature, capacity, and ability of our awareness, we conceive and bring forth our beliefs from inner forces. This can take many generations, but we always have among us advanced and inspired souls capable of comprehending new ideas more rapidly. Then, we have the masses who eventually come around to accepting arrangements of consciousness which look like any kind of advantage. Last, there are the laggards who only respond very slowly, and are most loth to alter whatever they have managed to assimilate.

We are now beginning to get a picture of how a Tradition is built. First, there are the agile, active and adventurous types who respond to inner energies by formulating and arranging them into a functional pattern. These formulations spread slowly among the less creative stratas of people and, in time, even the least responsive segments of humanity absorb this formalized energy. All the while, however, individuals are "feeding back" to this source energy which has been modified and adapted by their own experience. This means a steady and consistent development over a prolonged period. Therefore, the deepest levels of a Tradition are not static, but evolve at a rate relative to the chain of lives which alter it. This should result in a consistent improvement over the centuries which ought to show up ultimately as an overall advancement of human awareness and character, provided that clear contact has been faithfully maintained between the Life-levels throughout the whole time.

It is difficult for the average Westerner to appreciate the lengthy process which results in the building of a stable spiritual Tradition. Generations are born with percentages of this awareness scattered among them, but during their earth lives, it focuses in different forms from which feedback returns through channels of consciousness connected to the source of supply. As individuals die, their animating energy passes back along inner lines toward genetic points from which a return is very probable. Those reincarnating from that point will naturally take back traces of their Tradition in their genes, modified only to the slightest degree according to their own limitations. Thus the cycle goes on and on through the ages.

Historically, it appears that conflicting creeds and customs spring up, experience a period of popularity, then fade or disappear altogether. In fact, these are merely the outward appearance of formalized energies arising from a common level of Tradition as interpreted individually or collectively. However we think of them, they are but partial or transitory projections from a Tradition brought up for the conscious convenience of particular epochs or types of souls. Underneath, in the so-called "Unconscious", there exists an unbroken Tradition bound up with our spiritual survival. In effect, a Tradition could be described as a directional flow of Life-force from one generation to another, along definite lines of inner evolution, with the objective of establishing a state of immortal identity among Mankind. Perhaps Traditions might be termed channels of Cosmic continuity. Anyone able to identify himself into a Tradition may look back and say: "I came that way; that is me as I was," and equally looking forwards say: "That is me as I am going to be eventually." Such should be the spiritual value of a Tradition to human beings.

Normally, most humans are not objectively conscious of their Traditions, or their own significance within them. Any involvement with these deeper levels are generally subconscious and relatively insignificant. Nevertheless, in time these amass into appreciable contributions. The two extremes of humanity most keenly aware of their inner inheritance are those whose consciousness evolves slowest or fastest. At one end we have the typical countryman of any century, and at the other we find the intense innovator of ideas and the seeker of inspiration from the farthest spiritual sources. One looking earthward, the other toward the stars, we might think of them as Peasant and Poet. Between them, they hold the extremes of human Tradition, yet both are essential to its progression.

The value of the slow-changing Peasant is that he maintains the essential "body" of a Tradition in this world for long periods. This gives successive generations the opportunity to pick up keys from the past quickly and adapt them to contemporary living. It is the Peasant who preserves and prolongs our highest heritage in the humblest way. Nevertheless, this is insufficient in itself, and with no more stirring stimulus, a Tradition would stultify and stagnate. Prevention of that possibility is the task of our Poets—a classification to be taken in its broadest sense since they reach far out into spiritual space and return with enrichments of experience. These will eventually integrate into the Tradition he serves and lift it that much higher toward its ultimate target. By himself, the Poet might do no more than contact such spiritual spheres for his own benefit. Yet, through the Traditions kept alive by his less adventurous brethren, the Poet's advances and excursions into the broad spectrums of spiritual life are channelled for providing constant benefits to fellow mortals.

All this gives us a nice picture of a living Tradition. The "Peasantry" faithfully preserves the past, "Poets" explore for the future, and plain "People" are concerned with the needs of "Now". We live the same way ourselves for our short lifetimes, if we equate "Peasant" with the principle of Body, "People" with Mind, and "Poet" with Soul, taking "Tradition" to be the Spirit behind our being alive at all.

The vital two-way connections between our ordinary consciousness and the spiritual stream of our inner Traditions are effected by whatever means make common contacts with both states of our existence. That is to say, whatsoever of an objective nature has a subjective significance capable of linking up with our deepest levels of life. Or conversely anything of a purely spiritual nature translatable into terms of objective human living. Theoretically, of course, any part of our material universe has its spiritual counterpart and vice versa, but here we are looking for specific linkages which will lead straight from one area of awareness to the other. That limits our field at once to what could be described as "cultural", inclusive of religious, intellectual, and similar spheres of human adaption with the non-physical proportion of our existence. Moreover, we have to use suitable selections which are in keeping with the keynotes of the Tradition we are following. In our case, this would mean our outer conduct within the Western Tradition has to harmonize with its inner spiritual specifics if we are to live it with any degree of success.

Suppose we consider for a moment what a cultural field amounts to. It is a summation of human attempts at relationship with inner living realities by means of consciously contrived symbolism. Furthermore, by intentional arrangement of its integrals, it achieves a distinctive nature of its own epitomising that of its constructors. Therefore, the most direct contacts with our own Traditions come through cultural channels closest to our intrinsic states of selfhood. It is making the right relationships with and through these which presents all the problems and perplexities we are likely to meet with as followers of the Western Way.

The main elements of human culture are easily classifiable according to the three main stems or Pillars supporting the Tree of Life. Emotional arts to one side, intellectual pursuits to the other side, and purely spiritual aspirations in the middle. Sometimes these are called the Orphic path of emotion on the right, the Hermetic Path of intellect on the left, and the Mystic Path of direct Human-Divine relationship in the center. Considered as cultural streams, we experience them as our artistic, scientific, and religious heritage as they apply in their broadest sense to the theme of the Tradition itself.

Defining the actual "theme" of a Tradition is extremely difficult. Through the ages, a Tradition establishes the basics, then gradually picks up and accumulates an ever increasing mass of inner energy related to those basics. These combine into a kind of harmonic frequency or "keynote" which becomes the "Theme." It is this theme which determines the appropriate accretions, depletions, variants, or stabilizers necessary to keep the Tradition in a continuous state of spiritual integrity. We do much the same thing individually as our bodies take in quantities of consumables, sort out required nutrients, and eliminate the rest. Our minds and souls should function the same way. As we grow and learn we develop overall "life-themes" which determine what we build into our systems and what we have no affinity with. That is exactly what a Tradition does over a far longer period, because it is constructed by humans out of themselves as they live along lines of inner existence not limited to single incarnations.

This brief description shows how Inner Tradition in the West became established and how it continues to serve our spiritual needs. It is based on the sanctity of individual evolution toward a perfected state of being, and symbolized by "Illumination" and ultimate union with a Cosmo-Conception which has been called "Perfect Peace Profound". To that end, it is constructed through channels of culture and consciousness which accord with such a continuing theme from one generation to another. It develops through innovations by the few, adaptions by the many, and conservations among the multitudes. Its most important function is to provide us with the facilities for achieving a state of immortal identity with a higher condition of being.

Possibly the most intriguing method of establishing conscious contact with our Inner Tradition comes under the general heading of "Magic." This includes virtually all available cultural channels deriving its elements from every conceivable approach. It links the arts, sciences, crafts, beliefs, and emotional and intellectual abilities; in fact, the whole field of Western consciousness. Individuals may have only fractional powers in these areas, but the overall coverage amounts to quite an impressive inner total.

Despite the encyclopedic knowledge and wide practical experience of Western magical practitioners, there are few visible "teachers" of the subject itself. Where are the Western equivalents of the Mahatmas, Gurus and Masters of the Oriental tradition? How is it we do not find instructors of magic arts just as we meet those of musical, dramatic, literary, or any other art? How can a sincere seeker make contact with someone both willing and able to guide him or her along the Western Inner Way?

Our Secret Tradition is not something which can be learned from the lips or writings of any one person, nor can it be taught like a technical skill. Each aspirant must *evoke it out of himself*, through inner contacts with higher levels of consciousness which directly involve such supra-mundane matters. Strictly speaking, nobody can *tell* anyone else precisely how to do this. All a teacher can impart is information concerning how he thought he did it on his own account, which may or may not help whoever he is speaking to. What is more important is his ability to actually mediate inner contacts with our "spiritual superiors" so that those on lower levels may absorb this influence almost instinctively and translate it later into terms they understand in their own way.

In other words, a genuine "Teacher" of the Western Inner Way need not actually utter a single word in order to pass on his power. A state of shared consciousness which is linked through the "Teacher" or mediator to the correct inner contacts is sufficient. Everything depends on this mediative ability of a human soul to link the highest and lowest side of its nature so that others aware of the latter may benefit from the influence of the former. Either someone has developed this faculty in himself to an extent where others are able to appreciate it—or he has not. Those who have this ability may be considered true "Teachers" of our Tradition, but those who have not can still be regarded as informers or instructors concerning its purely academic points.

Therefore, it is perfectly possible for someone to talk of Western Traditional topics either with another person or a whole audience without actually *teaching* a single spiritual thing. Conversely, it is possible to contact someone who "passes on the Tradition" while simply sitting together in silence, or perhaps during a quite casual conversation or some shared amusement. In fact, it is only this inner mediation which really communicates our Tradition at all. It cannot be passed on by any amount of talk. We can speak about its symbolism, history, folklore, music, customs, or anything else about its external characteristics, but the Tradition itself is something purely spiritual and is transmitted by inner contact alone.

Most people "pick it up as they go", a little bit at a time from many sources. Not only from other souls, but also from creatures and creations of all kinds. Tradition comes these days as an absorbed accumulation of inner impressions received through media. There are very few other ways open whereby it could reach most of mankind. In order to both communicate and inform intelligently about it, someone would have to spend half a lifetime in close and conscious contact with the inner workings of the

Western Tradition. What percentage of our people have done this? One? Probably not nearly that many. One in several thousand is much more likely. Those few souls will scarcely seek intimate contacts with more than a strictly limited circle of associates. So the chances of an ordinary enquirer meeting a really initiated member of the Western Inner Way are very small. In any case, a direct contact would be of no use unless the enquirer already had an ability to absorb what was being mediated.

To think of "Masters" teaching eager pupils all the arts of magic for their personal gain is totally unrealistic. As a matter of interest, the words "Master", "Teacher", or similar terms indicating spiritual superiority are no longer used in Western initiated circles. Those so describing themselves would be outside those areas. No sincere soul, aware of his connection with the Western Inner Way, considers himself higher, better, or worth more than his fellow beings. He is simply increasingly conscious of his obligations to Life and accepts a greater responsibility towards the Spirit and every species thereof. It does not intend to "master" anyone except itself. All it can conscientiously offer to others willing themselves along the same Way is companionship. Thus, a designation of "Companion" would be the only acceptable title among modern initiates of the Western Inner Way.

Despite all this, it is still valid to say: "When the pupil is ready the Master will appear." When someone has reached the state of consciousness needed to receive some specific information this will automatically attract the means of supplying such an inner need. The "Master", or supplier of that information could be anything from the printed page to a passing stranger. We must be prepared to accept what comes in whichever way it is able to contact us. The first requirement is to create an inner state of need without demanding absurd replies in the shape of exalted personages offering their exclusive services for the sake of our personal edification. Replies will indeed reach us—sometimes under very strange circumstances—but recognition and acceptance of them is strictly a personal decision.

Therefore, the sooner seekers of the Western Inner Tradition set aside ideas of mysterious "Masters" arriving out of the blue to teach them every trick of the magical trade, the better progress we shall make together. Insofar as there are actual "Teachers" of our Tradition, these are beings existing on inner, though connected, dimensions. It is true we have individual incarnate souls with us on earth who mediate influences from those and higher sources. Some are able to do this constantly, and others only very occasionally. The essential thing to learn early in Western inner workings is that we should never expect wonderful "messages" in terms of words, and to seeking instead experiences of inner life itself, translatable through the symbology of our spiritual systems. This may be an unpalatable lesson, but until it is properly understood there will be little progress made along Western Pathways.

It is sometimes a surprising thing at the end of an incarnation wherein no meeting with magical Masters seemed evident, to realize suddenly these were really there all the time. A few seconds of contact here, a touch somewhere else, an unforgettable impact occasionally, and a steady subconscious background all the while from somewhere too deep for ready recognition. So long as we are willing to learn the inner side of our lives, we shall never be left without guidance. Western "Masters" do not "teach" Tradition by speaking, writing, or lecturing, or through other forms of conventional communication. They mediate its Living spirit for their fellow souls. The deeper that fact of inner life penetrates the awareness of would-be "pupils" the better for them and the rest of us.

Another important point to grasp is that our Inner Tradition in itself is not magic *per se*, but a purely spiritual substratum of our existence reachable to different degrees by many ways. What we classify as magic is mainly a systemized process of applied consciousness and behaviour calculated to touch our Tradition as deeply and truly as we may. Mankind has understood and practised magic under so many names, and with such a variety of forms that it may be very difficult to appreciate its influence and necessity in our modern lives. To help us see this issue a little more plainly, let us study some of the principles explaining how we relate ourselves and our Inner Tradition in a magical manner through spiritual symbolism.

2. Symbolic Significance

In primitive times, there was little distinction between religion and magic in establishing relationships with inner life. Those who instinctively felt the presence of invisible causative powers behind the objective world reacted according to inclination and made patterns that eventually turned into time-honored traditional tracks. The divergence of magic from religion depended on individual or collective attitudes towards whatever "THAT" might be which seemed to determine human destiny. There were not many alternative attitudes which could very well be adopted. Mainly they were:

1. Assume some God—or Gods—capable of everything. It would therefore pay humans to worship and placate such a Being with everything they could think of. Most religions grew out of this attitude.

2. Assume the same Being or Beings, but believed it possible to work out some kind of mutual arrangements with It or Them. That is to say, find common grounds for a partnership between Humanity and Divinity. The basics of magic came from that approach.

3. Ignore the whole idea and get on with living in this world

for whatever can be got out of it whether there are Gods or not. The bulk of human behavior comes from this category.

From a compromise between 1 and 2, Philosophy later entered the field with an attitude of: "Who knows what is or isn't, but its fine to try finding out."

From 3 came a commerce-hardened core of cynicism saying: "The best thing to do with Gods is buy them out and run the whole racket for a pretty profit."

Eventually there were many other sub-divisions, but on the whole, the main difference between Western religion and magic is a question of human dependency. Broadly speaking, religion claims that man is entirely and utterly dependent on God, cannot save himself by his own efforts, and has to rely on Divinity for everything. Magic believes in Divinity, but postulates that the same Laws of Life bind mortals and immortals alike. Therefore, some compromise of consciousness should be possible between them.

Of these two basic approaches, magic is much more individualistic than religion, and as human intellect widened, philosophy opened up independent observation. Once more it became the collectivism versus individualism question. "Am I self-sufficient enough to be my own authority or not?" Perhaps, in the most primitive way: "Am I a Herder or a Hunter?" Official religion tended to the viewpoint "Let's all stick together for the sake of safety and mutual advantage." Magic, being always unofficial, went the opposite way and insisted: "In important enterprises, small circles of companions who can totally rely upon each other are best. But, in the long run, everyone has to depend on his own efforts." Philosophy waved tolerant hands in every direction and exhorted everyone to sort things out whichever way they could, offering all kinds of suggestions and encouragement for free selection.

Before the main stream of migration to the West in search of spiritual independence, humans had constructed quite complicated systems of symbolism for relating metaphysical values with material life on earth. Symbols have always been a medium for exchanging conscious energies. We would have no form of communication with each other without them. Written or spoken words are symbols. So are signs, gestures, numbers, or anything what ever which is intended to carry and relate consciousness between people. Some are universally acknowledged, while others become limited to more and more exclusive circles. Eventually we come to secret codings which include the most intimate and important symbols of all. One is the single genetic code which distinguishes each individual being in existence, and the other is that which identifies Ultimate Entity Itself. Those were symbolised in both religious and magical circles by individual "secret names" and the "Great Unknowable Name of God."

From the esoteric perspective, when someone came to know their own identity-name it would unify them with the Ultimate Name and another individual life would have reached Perfection. That means that if anyone could actually become exactly what they were meant to be by their own unique genetic coding, they would automatically have no more need to exist outside of Divine Perfection. Hence, the concern of many souls to seek that Identity by every possible means. The "Wild Hunt" was certainly on in the West, and the initial objective was a suitable symbology to carry our type of Tradition toward its individual destiny.

The "Wild Hunt" idea is one of our earliest esoteric symbols. According to the legend, all departed souls in the West duly waited at appointed stations to be collected once a year at Samhain, "All Souls Night". This was overseen by Gwyn ap Nudd (Light, Son of Darkness) in his chariot, accompanied by immortal companions on horseback and a whole pack of huge white hounds with glowing red eyes. The dogs made sure no one was lost or forgotten. A chief pick-up place in West Britain was the top of Gastonbury Tor. "Tor" not only stands for a high hill, but also means Door, or Gateway. Gwyn apparently took every soul with him for sorting out at the end of their celestial journey. Opinions varied as to what happened then, but there was general agreement they all got whatever they rightly deserved.

To see this typically Western symbol in its best light, transpose its elements. Take individual souls as the hunters, and Gwyn ap Nudd as the "Divine Spark" or Inner Identity we should all seek in ourselves. We hunt him (IT) with our white hounds (true thoughts) with red eyes (which see through deceptive darkness), and we are accompanied by mounted friends (fellow seekers by the same system). Gwyn is to be met at the apex of a Holy Hill where Earth and Sky meet, at the critical poising point where the very top of our human nature meets the lowest levels of our higher being. Moreover, Gwyn only comes once a year, meaning we have at least one good chance in every incarnation to make this vital inner contact, and if we miss that magic moment we shall have to wait for the next opportunity. There is still plenty to learn from the legend if anyone is interested enough to do more digging. Bear in mind that early Western Traditionalists often moved elements of their magical myths around so that only initiated minds could follow the story along inner levels.

Westernizing mankind, looking for new spiritual symbolism, found it in the beautiful simplicity of natural items that suggested qualities of inner actualities. Every tree, plant, flower, rock, animal, or bird, became a symbol of an arcane language. Later, these evolved into totemistic family identifications, and later still gave rise to the art of heraldry. What is particularly interesting about the early symbology of the West is that no large and imposing idols appear to have been erected in public temples. Not until Roman times did official images of national deities appear in Western Europe. Odd cult figures turned up occasionally, but esoteric symbolism consisted principly of geometric designs, markings, gestures, hill-calls, and other natural things. To these were attached significance only interpretable by initiated intelligence.

It almost seemed as if the emerging West was determined to leave Oriental intricacies and elaborations behind and use only aesthetically pure and simple spiritual symbology. There has always been a dislike of over-embellishment or flamboyancy in the Western Way. Compare even today the simple style of English churches with the elaborations of Eastern Orthodox ones. Periodically, there have been odd flare-ups about ceremonial complications. The most noticeable was the Reformation when so many people were objecting to what they considered "alien" religious influences. They asked for simpler rites in their own language. Even those were eventually too much for succeedingly "lower" generations of churchgoers, who became more independent in outlook and demanded starker symbology until the brick wall and bare bench meeting houses brought the cycle to a rather miserable state of stagnation. This was Western Traditionalism in one of its most awkward moods.

The esoteric or magical branch of the Tradition followed

patterns similar to the religious branch. Symbology started out simply, but eventually developed curious complications of its own along inner lines. Metaphors and euphemisms twisted around and around until guessing what initiates were talking about turned into a major mental game. This was, again, "the great hunt." Its symbols and language became incorporated into magical practice. The implements of the hunt, the dagger or arrow, spear or staff, shield, horn, and length of cord, became the Magical Instruments of the Western Tradition.

We can trace those same symbols yet—attached to the typical image of a Western cowboy. The old spear has become his gun—carbine or hand. The sword or dagger has shrunk to a bowie knife, and the shield turned to "chaps", a protective leather riding apron. Horns changed to the powder flasks for muzzle-loaders, and can also be considered as water-bottles. The cord, of course, is hanging on the saddle as a lassoo. Another type of rope was woven purely from horsehair and had an extremely useful purpose. It was laid in a circle round men sleeping on the open ground where snakes were likely to be moving at night. No snake would crawl across a horsehair rope because the stiff hairs stuck between their scales and hurt them. Thus we get a symbolic picture of a man in his magic circle, safe against the intrusions of evil. Often, the men were guards of a horned herd on their way to sacrifice. The almost magical aura surrounding cowboys stems very much from our deeply inherent sacred symbolism.

Most magical practice grew from quite commonplace acts of specialized skill. Take the symbolic protective circle traced around practitioners of traditional Western magic. It was often outlined with the end of a tall staff while the operator stood in the center. Sometimes the staff was set upright in the ground while the operator scraped the circle with the point of a knife which was attached to the staff by a cord. This was, in fact, the preliminary act of making a primitive hunter's hut or shelter. Once the circle had been traced, fresh cut ash staves were pushed into the ground at even intervals around it, then bent inwards and tied to the center pole. This provided a strong frame to be covered with skins or maybe more solidly finished off with wattle and daub. The end product was a hunter's home, and what else is the inner meaning of a magical circle?

While the men were hunting meat, the women were mostly hunting herbs. Properties of these were discovered the hard way—eat them and see. If people started dropping dead or were violently sick, then those herbs were reserved for enemies. The womenfolk thus collected considerable herbal skills which they passed down in strict confidence to their daughters. It was necessary to know how to feed a family when father failed to bring home the bacon, but it could also come in useful to know what would get rid of the brute if he cut up too rough and too often! Abortion was another fine art to be mistress of. So was experience of what we now call hallucinogens, analgesics, and a few other herbal pharmaceuticals. The entire basis of what was later called "witchcraft" was built on knowledge and application of vegetable poisons. No wonder people were instinctively terrified of it! A single malicious witch in a community could poison everyone with a bit of this and that in the communal cooking pot. She might also kill off their cattle or spread blight on their crops. Witches were bad magic of the worst kind.

On the good side, of course, were women who only used their herbal knowledge to help their families and friends. Everything depended on motivation. When hunters got badly hurt, it was their womenfolk who treated their wounds. On the other hand, if someone were dying with difficulty and in great pain, it was a kindly act to give him a fatal drink to induce coma and death. So it might be to terminate the pregnancy of a terrified girl who had been raped. As well as herb brews, the women knew the value of making soothing sounds not only to babies, but troubled adults in the throes of emotional sufferings. Rhythmic hand strokings accompanied by sympathetic and hypnotic croonings worked wonders with what we now call psychosomatic problems. As these became stylized they were handed down through families as traditional "spells". The gentle gibberish of the "words" may have meant nothing very special, but the person-to-person direct application meant everything.

Eventually, the good and bad of the magical women became symbolized by the bush and the besom, both linked with pubic hair. The "witches" broom was not only a weapon wielded by an ill-tempered woman, but its hand polished handle could be used for masturbation and sex stimulation practices. So it became the sign of a socially wicked woman. (Still called a "besom" in some country places). The "bush" on the other hand, was a bunch of healing herbs and, some thought better still, brewing herbs. Brewing the heady concoction of grain in which herbs were steeped was a female accomplishment appreciated by every man. Nobody knows for certain when brewers began tying the herbs to a long pole and sticking it up outside the house so that it could plainly be seen by everyone to tell them: "Beer up!" in unmistakable symbology. Definitely, all the local boozers thought it a wonderful sign of a woman trying to make men happy.

In addition to their pharmacology and other gifts, the women, or rather a few specialists among them, were prophetesses, clairvoyants and, as we say nowadays, sensitives. These were the ones who did most of the direct conscious communication with other levels of life. In common with pythonesses of earlier times, western women mainly made their inspired utterances in very veiled symbology. Sometimes they only gave vent to shrieks and queer cries and groans. Quite often, this by itself was sheer rubbish. Yet, in attempting to seek some intelligible meaning, those listening could occasionally push their own inner perceptions to points where sense came to them from other channels. Here and there, however, really talented women must have given very valuable guidance which has subtly altered the course of our history. Throughout our whole tradition there have been instances of women bringing strange messages and tidings from other and inner worlds which influenced people in this one. None of this seemed due to any special training or teachings, but to a purely genetic or inherent faculty usually running in families, but only appearing in every other generation in rare instances.

We have to remember that magicians have mothers, and in bygone times they learned their elementary symbology during early childhood from their mothers and grandmothers. It was not uncommon for boys who seemed too fragile or unfit for what were considered proper male pursuits to be brought up by womenfolk. With them, the child picked up all the semi-secret lore customarily passed on to daughters, but he dealt with this through his masculine type of consciousness. A long time ago, some unknown little boy watched his mother winding a ball of wool and noted how it grew so neatly and evenly because each circuit was wound at a cross angle to the last. Eventually, he or associates came to realize how the Cosmos theoretically comes together from its Time-Space-Event components, and the cross-angled triple circle of the Cosmos symbol was conceived. For that reason, a ball of wool or twine became a major magical symbol of the Celts. Many centuries later, another little boy watched his mother's kettle boiling, and steam symbolized an energy which is still with us.

It is during the child's formative years that magical symbols make their maximum impression, building a background to live against for the rest of an incarnation. They tend to awaken an awareness stemming from long-ago lives and conditions of consciousness away from this world. In adolescence, the same symbols will take on a sexual significance and evoke creativeness (or perhaps contrariness!) with considerable vigor. Later, the symbols will lead more steadily toward the integration of an individuality arising out of incarnation. Lastly, these same symbols take on a different significance of survival beyond embodiment pointing toward the future in another and hopefully higher condition of consciousness. Perhaps it is not so strange that many people who, in early middle life, were disbelievers in immortality find their views altering as their incarnations come to a close. In late life, magical symbolism becomes a matter of deep and quiet conviction rather than something sensational or spectacular.

A noticeable difference between religious and magical symbolic formulas is that the former usually crystalize into set liturgical procedures with standard interpretations, while the latter are far more fluid and mobile. Magical rituals were not written or stage-set until recently, and then there was little to look at of much solid value. The magic of earlier epochs was frequently of an impromptu nature. There was a general understanding of what had to be done during any specific proceedings, but a lot of individual items were verbalized or acted according to the enlightenment of whoever was working them. There were alternative ways of employing the same symbols in different localities, for instance, and various circles had their own carefully guarded "code-calls" for connecting with inner aware-ness. While Western religion was concerned with standardizing its symbology and co-ordinating its members by means of hierarchial methods, Western magic was being more than liberal in free interpretative expressions of basic symbolism and radical relationships with inner life.

It is significant that Western magic has never had an earthly established hierarchy dominating its strucutre with authoritarian rulings. That would be entirely contrary to our Inner Tradition. There is, however, a *spiritual* hierarchy "behind the scenes" which links the magical members of the Tradition together through inner channels of consciousness. Again and again various ambitious attempts have been made to establish hierarchial magical power-structures. Each time they have broken apart and disintegrated. There is a certain "critical mass" which magical co-operatives of the West can hold together harmoniously and after that point is passed, it seems groupings start to fall apart. Our Tradition is geared to an arrangement of separate units in this world connected and co-related into inner unity by a non-material membership. The maximum number of physical coherence seems to be twelve.

Most people these days think of thirteen as the number of a witch-coven, but in fact it has always been the basis of Western magical associations. The whole point is that only twelve people were *humans*. They groups around the *invisible* member forming their inner nucleus, and that is how they held together if they were compatible. The construction figure is arrived at by the principle that a perfect sphere will need just twelve spheres of its size to cover its surface in equal contact with it and each other. In other words, twelve is a natural harmonic relatively to a unit. Nothing more mystical than that. The idea of thirteen being unlucky applies only if the thirteenth person is human, because that would be tantamount to taking the rightful place of a God—a risky impertinence for all concerned.

In later times among some of the degenerated gatherings a "God" was personified by a masked human usually in horned guise. By then, ancestral memories of Sacred King and animal life-sacrifices were getting dim and dingy. The pagan peasant part of our Tradition kept ancient symbology going in very muddled and downgraded ways perhaps, but it was all they knew how to handle, and they were not very willing to purify or clean up customs which satisfied their senses and hit out at hated authorities a few times a year. Sooner or later they would have to haul themselves up the Ladder of Life a bit and start reconstructing their rituals on better lines of behavior. So long as there is a residue of fundamental symbolism to work with, reconstitution of original meanings in modern terms will always be possible.

Although there has always been a Western spiritual symbology, it did not start condensing into summative Master-symbols until we had been working with it for quite a few centuries. Our oldest and most sacred Sign of this nature is the Cosmic Cross. Common to all traditions one way or another, it has differing interpretations, and Western magic settled for the now well-known arrangement quite a while back. Inwardly, it is our Compass of Consciousness steering our unseen course through Cosmos. Outwardly it is the Compass of Direction without which we could not travel around territory or navigate the oceans. Christianity later added the sign of Man to it, but officially dispensed with the circle, possibly because non-Christian gatherings had always assumed that natural formation. The esoteric West resented that high-handed interference with basic beliefs very much indeed, and "Celtic" Crosses are still with us. To this day, the special "consecration crosses" on Christian altars and churches are the old Cosmic type of quartered circles.

Eventually, our Tradition produced the great Symbols conjoining consciousness with the various spiritual streams; The Grail, The Tree of Life, The Rose Cross, The Square and Compass and others. Each is an aegis providing a magical connection with appropriate parts of the Western Inner Way. For we have not only extended and diversified ourselves on earth, but inwardly as well. Our varying soul-types need suitable spiritual structures and accommodation according to their states and conditions of development. All are catered for under the heading of one Western symbol or another, and if totally new needs should arise in the future, then we must evolve more master-signs covering such expansions of our tradition.

In the earlier days of the West, practically everything became a symbol that meant something in mystic language. The inner-life could be reached to some degree through all natural things and most artifactual ones. Innumerable dictionaries have been compiled on various aspects of Western symbology, including birds, beasts, trees, plants, designs, tools, and much more. We were put in contact with inner consciousness wherever we went and with almost anything we used. There was a whole wealth of significance in ordinary kitchen utensils. The cauldron, the knife, the ladle, the whetstone, pieces of string—they all had their secret stories which the children learned little by little as they grew up. It was a very enriching experience sadly absent among recent generations. Imagine a modern mother finding a single mystic meaning behind her fridge, food-mixer, electric fry pan, and shiny saucepans. Her kids are dumped in front of a television. Do they get as much out of it as their young ancestors did from great-great-great-great-grandmother's tales while they watched the flickering flames throw shadow shows all over the wall.

Nowadays, we Westerners are apt to ignore inner signals from our environment and keep to the relatively few locked up in Lodges or Temples, whether real or figurative. Now and then we let some of our symbols out, play with them a while, then put them back until next time. One day, more than a few people are going to wonder what they seem to be missing in everyday life and start looking for something to fill that sense of vacancy. They need not look very far. Inside themselves they have a whole Tradition trying to come out and live through everything in their existence. It only takes a deep enough call to summon its symbols into close conscious contact.

Maybe some minds will direct critical attention to the magical or masonic Lodges and Temples which employ much of our arcane Western symbolism. Externally they appear as a lot of little men and women trying to magnify themselves with make-believe, just as they did when children. Except, of course, that they now wear much more expensive decorations, give themselves more exotic titles, and go through more solemn antics laid down in their books as correct ritual procedures. How far are they fooling themselves if they do not know how to use their symbolism properly? Are they actually using it for reaching back into their own inner depths and contacting their real identities? Or are they only having fun with their wish-wantings and fantasies for the sake of escapist enjoyment? No one could answer that except themselves—if they realized the inner realities involved.

To succeed with magical symbolism it has to be pushed quite a long way past the lower levels of self-life and beyond the personality. It may then contact inner realities connected to a sense of identification with Life as an immortal Spirit. That is no easy exercise, but a magical maneuver demanding a lot more effort, determination, and sacrifice than most average people might be prepared to offer. Sacrifice is a frightening word in modern ears, yet it is the rock bottom symbol of our tradition. That is what lies behind and underneath all our magic, religion, beliefs, and behaviors as Western people. Perhaps we should go back to our beginnings again and learn something about how our sacrificial Sacred Kings started us on the path we should be following.

3. The Sacred Self-Sacrifice

Right at the very foundation of our Western Inner Tradition rises the majestic figure of the Slain Sacred King. He is the archetype of "one who dies that many may live," the acme of individualization into immortality. Most people have various ideas about Sacred Kings being slain to appease Divine Wrath, promote fertility, and such, but the remotest origins of this practice are not sufficiently realized. To understand, we have to put ourselves in the place of our most primitive ancestors and see life through their eyes.

Trying to survive in a hostile world with no better weapons than sharp stones and sticks, was a very desperate affair. Little tribes of a few families struggling to exist on natural resources knew this only too well. In warm climates, lush vegetation, fruits, small reptiles, off-shore fish and molluscs would mostly provide a living. Venturing into colder territory, where winter cut off so many supplies, was another matter. The only answer to starvation then was meat, which had to be caught on the hoof and eaten raw until the art of fire-handling was learned.

In those days, herd animals with the most meat to offer were quite wild. They stampeded easily and either trampled attackers to death or escaped from them. Man could not outrun or outfight them, so he had to outwit them. Early hunters probably noted how beasts of prey would stalk herd creatures carefully until able to creep close, select a victim, make one huge spring for its neck. By that time the rest of the herd had gone, but the carcass provided meat to feed the predator and family for maybe several days. This seemed practical enough for a creature with powerful muscles, sharp fanges, and long claws, but how could humans, with their inferior armament, hope to compete?

Eventually, experience taught them. The most powerful, agile, and skilled hunter among them impersonated a herd animal in order to creep close enough to one for a kill. This he did by wearing the skin and horns taken from some previous kill. In that way he looked and smelt vaguely familiar to his prey. In order to lull their suspicions even more, the hunter moved as much like them as possible, and imitated their noises as best he could. His weapons were only a sharpened stabbing stick or a jagged stone. Otherwise, he had to depend on his own speed and strength.

When the fatal moment came, the hunter had to leap suddenly on the back of a startled animal and hang there with feet and one hand while he stabbed frantically into flesh with the other, hoping to hit a vital spot. How often the man slew the beast or lost his life in the attempt is anyone's guess. The point is that some hunters certainly succeeded, and their friends and families then had meat to eat, skin to wear, and bones to make tools with. Chances are that casualty rates among such hunters were very high indeed. Even if not killed, they must have frequently been maimed for the rest of their lives. Only direst necessity drove them to take the risk.

Meanwhile, the mythos had begun. Sacred kingship was instituted among mankind as a salvation-pattern, growing up quite naturally from the Hunter-heros. The story evolved something like this: First there had to be a people in desperate need of something, without which they would certainly perish. They prayed and prayed, saying "Who will save us?" From among them came forth a young man full of strength and ability who assured them, "I am he you seek. I will get what you need to save you from death even though it costs my own life. All I ask is that you think of me and remember what I have done so that I shall live on among you in spirit." The people blessed him thankfully, because it seemed to them some supernatural power had entered him. So he set out alone on his hazardous quest and succeeded in gaining what his people needed, in this case food. The effort cost him his life, but true to their promise, the people praised his name and remembered what he had done for them. Even while they ate the flesh and drank the blood of his donation, it seemed to them that somehow they were partaking of their dead savior also. They thought of him lovingly and admiringly as they told their children: "He died so that we and you might live. Some of you must do the same when your turn comes."

Later on there were more ways young heroes might die to save their people than providing them with food. They might fight off some fierce marauder or hostile humans while their folk escaped. However they met their ends, it was always in the service of their folk family so that others might carry on the line of life they shared among them. In return, they were duly honored and admired and became part of the legend which their people were living together. The debt owed them was never forgotten, but passed deeply down the generations until it became a sense of Divinity itself. Their images grew with the telling into Savior figures of a perilous past whose spirits would be with their people always, arising again and again to defend them against dangers.

We have to remember that primitive people were matriarchally minded. For them, the Mother Archetype was a universal producer and provider, but great as She was, her gifts had to be taken the hard way in most cases. Mothers could be cruel or kind, and She was certainly both. Being female, mothers loved strong sons, and the strong sons of men must therefore be favorites of the Great Mother. When they died, She would replace them in Her womb and bring them back to life again. She could send them back to women's wombs among their people once more, and they might rejoin those who loved them on earth and would welcome their return. Resurrection was as simple as that.

So, for the folk-hero of early times, death was a way back to life again. He was assured of a return ticket in advance; not only that, but a privileged position among his people into the bargain. Therefore, he was acting in his own best interests when he gave his life for the sake of his fellows. Dying a savior, he could be reborn a king. All this because he was willing to individuate himself in an outstanding way. Physical death seemed a small price to pay for such glory.

Over the centuries, the mystique of the Sacred King grew indissolubly into both the foundation and theme of our Tradition. It alone explains why Christianity became popular in the West. "The Man who died and became God and would return again as King" was no new theme for folk in the first century A.D. It was their Old Religion back again, despite new-fangled and sophisticated theologies that temple priests had been proclaiming and promoting for the sake of profit and power. No wonder Christianity caught on so fast among common people who remembered genetically the folk-faith of olden times. For them, Jesus was an ancient symbol in a modern setting.

It is uncertain when the deaths of Sacred Kings ceased to be dire necessities, becoming purely religious ritual. As people grew more expert at hunting and began the practice of herd-keeping, the Sacred King's original function really became superfluous. So strong had the tradition become, however, that it continued through tribal consciousness in various forms right down the centuries until today. The ideal of self-sacrifice and courageous conduct is still held up as a behavior code to be admired and respected. Though young men are no longer expected to lay their bodies on altars, they are yet liable to die in defense of whatever State or economy they owe allegiance to by birth or adoption.

Most probably the ritualized sacrifice of Sacred Kings developed with the rise of what eventually became the priestly class. This would naturally be confined to those having keener or clearer insight than average, plus an ability to interpret what they felt and saw for the benefit of their kinfolk. To some extent at least, they must have formed associations among themselves as people do today who share common intellectual or spiritual levels. Having achieved an "apart from the mass" ability of inner vision, they began to recognize many of the mistakes mankind was making, not least of which was inbreeding. Results of inbreeding among small communities were becoming obvious, but the question was how to alter human habits and somehow introduce better blood into available stock. The only answer lay in obtaining imported seed, and impregnating a limited number of females belonging to the community. It was important to limit such offspring, otherwise all would be back to the beginning again.

Thus another type of Sacred King came to life. The terms of his office were, briefly, that he should leave his village, go far off (as much as fifty miles maybe) to the people who had chosen him, live with them for a year fertilizing their selected females, then accept a ceremonial death at the end of the term so that his blood-line would be limited. Of course there was the customary promotion to Godhood afterwards, and possibly a return ticket via a reincarnation. Naturally, he had to be in prime condition to start with, and have outstanding qualities setting him well above the average for his day and locality. He knew quite well what was expected of him and was only too willing to pay the price. His selection was a very great honor for his family. Blood relationship with a Sacred King was something to hold in the highest esteem. During his sacred service he might expect every kind of privilege and pleasure procurable, and at least he was assured a relatively merciful and quick death at the end. By that time his earliest begotten offspring would have arrived as evidence of his efficiency. Eventually, they would be mated with those begotten by the next Sacred King appointed, and so the stock was supposed to improve accordingly.

As might be anticipated, all kinds of customs and survivals became incorporated into this growing practice. In the past, both mime and music had been taught the hunter-kings as imitations of animal movements and noises. Those grew into sacred dances and religious chanting. It is possible that the deep bows made by priests before an altar even today originated in the head-down grazing motions made by ruminants content in each other's company. Perhaps the processionals yet with us derived from the measured plodding of beasts moving patiently along towards fresh pasturage. Time may alter the externals of a Tradition, but its fundamentals are always with us.

Even during the reign of the Fertility-King, the old hunters had grown to God-like proportions, becoming huge, horned, shadowy figures in the background of belief. Many people nowadays presume that the horned Gods were of an animal nature. This is not quite the case. They were, in fact, humans who had attained "Godhood" while wearing that guise, thus symbol-izing humanity achieving divinity through sacrifice. Quite apart from any phallic or other significance, the horned headdress has always signified the highest of human honors. Hebrews attributed a gift of horns to Moses. Their priestly mitres suggested horns like those of the later Christian bishops, which formed the outline of two horns meeting on top as a sign of the Trinity. Royal crowns outline four horns from a diadem meeting centrally. Altars of sacrifice are symbolically horned at the corners, and the word "corner" itself comes from "cornu", a horn. Though the Christ Figure is not obviously horned, the head is thorn-crowned as a symbol of suffering sacrifice instead. We should also remember the symbology of the Unicorn. An emblem of genetic purity, the Unicorn "lays its head in the lap of a Virgin", i.e. fertilizes her magically with its phallic horn. In esoteric Christian mythology this symbolizes the Incarnation of a Divine King, via the "immaculate conception". Artificial insemination might be a more modern interpretation.

Improved genetics resulted in not only better human stock, but occasionally outstanding individuals who made valuable contributions to human knowledge or culture. The priesthood felt convinced these were special souls sent in from higher spheres to help humanity. Sometimes they suspected that earlier Sacred Kings had reached some superior spiritual state and really returned with added wisdom and inner experience in order to teach and instruct their people. Thus opened up yet another aspect of Sacred Kingship—the Way-shower image.

There came a period when foodstuffs were relatively dependable and human breeding reasonable, yet the affairs of humanity still seemed desperate. Once more the services of the Sacred Kings were needed, this time as Teachers of Truth. The theory was that if suitable individuals were sacrificed in a correct manner, their souls would be taken in training by spiritual agencies. Later, these souls were sent back to this world with a mission of righting wrongs and showing folk how to set their muddles and mismanagements straight again. In order to keep up a supply of such teachers, there had to be a steady flow of sacrificial Kings available from the altars of this world.

By this time, with the coming of professional priesthood, Sacred King practices diverged a long way from their original mark. God-figures of awesome dimensions and human characteristics were emerging with demands that seemed suspiciously like those of their discoverers. They demanded worship, wealth, luxury, and control of all commodities, in return for which they would be graciously pleased to return percentages to the producers. On the whole, they could be benevolent providing those working for them acknowledged inferiority and dependence on this divine dispensation.

A natural query coming to most people's minds is why the sacrifice always seems exclusively male. Why no "Sacred Queen?" Originally, of course, because no woman was likely to posses the physical strength and speed needed to make a "hunter's kill." Then, in a matriarchy, the women were needed for breeding and controlling the tribal councils. Males were expected to die so that females lived. Today we theoretically have the "women and children first" tradition in an emergency. After all, one male can fertilize many females, but females can only produce one child per year. To repopulate a tribe quickly after some near wipe-out called for few males, but many females.

In one sense there was a Sacred Queen. The dedicated virgin whose job it was to call back the sacrificed King into her womb. At first this must have been a simple hope, wish, or maybe a choice of the man himself, requested at the last moment. He may have expected his own father or brother to bring him back to life by thinking and praying about him while engaged in a special sex act for the purpose. It is possible that the custom of a man putting a child into his dead brother's widow on behalf of the deceased was a relic of primitive resurrection practices. Later on, however, such hit and miss attempts were superseded by all kinds of elaborate ritual systems which may or may not have worked better. We have to remember that the first Sacred Kings served only very small human groupings. As communities grew larger, group participation in ritualized customs became far more formalized and complicated. This should have increased their technical efficiency, provided the intent and depth of spiritual sincerity was multiplied accordingly. At best the Sacred King was assured of the greatest possible trouble taken on his behalf, and at worst he realized a large audience was applauding his last appearance.

There seems little doubt that in many instances the literal flesh and blood of the sacrificed man was shared in fact among his immediate friends or a select circle of communicants; possibly only among those who were to play an immediate part in his resurrection process. By symbolically sharing his sacrifice they hoped to share his immortality. Nevertheless, increasing demands by the populace for closer contact with their saviours called for some gesture by the organizers, and so the practice of scattering blood drops over the people present grew more general. Those receiving a single spot were assured of salvation and others must have hoped they were included in the general gesture. People present at King Charles the First's public murder instinctively tried to dip handkerchiefs into his spilt blood. Tradition may seem dormant, but it never dies. To this day, the rather revolting practice of "blooding" the youngest child present at its "first kill" of a foxhunt persists. This is usually made by marking the child's forehead with the bloody stump of the fox's severed tail or "brush". In bygone times it would have been a brush of some sacred twigs dipped in the victim's blood and flicked out over the bowed heads of bystanders. Today a plastic holy-water caster has to simulate the symbology of blood- purification over the heads of the congregation at High Mass.

Looking back again over the principles of Sacred Kingship as practiced in olden times, there are many interesting points to consider. Maybe the most vital is the voluntary nature of the sacrifice. It had to be a one hundred percent act of free will on the part of the victim. Theoretically, the slightest compulsion or coercion applied would invalidate the act. Furthermore, although such freewill made the act technically into a suicide, the fatal stroke had to be given by the victim's own people in the person of their appointed slayer. So why should not a willing victim simply kill himself before witnesses?

The free-will element is reasonably obvious. To offer freely one's own body and blood was, and yet is, about the highest act of individualism imaginable to most mortals. Far from being "selfless", it asserts the acme of Self-hood. It says, in effect, "I do not need a common carcass to be *me*. I am capable of surviving as my spirit alone. Death does not diminish me, it deifies me. You, my people, are partners with me, and I will lead the way for you to follow along other paths. We will live together forever, because I offer my life for your sake. I shall be immortal among you always."

It is possible that during the earliest epochs Sacred Kings supposed they were simply safeguarding their own survival by giving their lives on behalf of their immediate families. If an entire group of people were wiped out, none of them would be able to get back earthwards again through their special line. That would be tantamount to being utterly defeated by other tribes and cast into captivity through the spirit world. To assert independence and achieve individuality, they had to keep at least a minimum of their line alive and active on earth. It was only commonsense that whoever set the highest value on this individualization should be willing to sacrifice a single incarnation for the sake of future attainments. In that way he was assured of his spiritual status for at least as long as his folk-family lasted.

The actual taking of his life with his own hands was impermissible for this reason. If he had done that himself, his people would not have been included in the sacrifice at all. It would have been limited to his individual life only and not another soul would be involved. Furthermore, he would have automatically closed the gate of his return among his people, and be lost to them forthwith. That was no help to anyone. No, the only noble and proper way out was by letting the people he loved deal the death-blow. That sealed the spiritual bond between them all forever. One might almost say "Greater love hath no man than this; that he lay down his life *to* his friends." It had to be his own people who took the life of a Sacred King, because those who took the life had a claim to the spiritual services of the soul so liberated. To be killed by other than his own people in a recognized ritual way would mean his spirit might have to serve those killers instead. Such was the fate of captured enemy prisoners who were butchered in bunches in the service of conquering gods. Sacred Kings died for the spiritual freedom of themselves and their folk. That made all the difference.

This raises some rather technical points concerning the Sacred Kingship of Jesus. He was not killed by the Jews but by the Romans. It was Pilate who ordered the title of "Rex Judaeorum" attached to the cross. In Pilate's time, this old description of "king" also applied to the sacred surrogate appointed to make sacrifices in the rulers' names on behalf of their people. Thus Pilate's official notice on the cross represented his own opinion about the nature of the Nazarene, an opinion he refused to alter on account of priestly pressure from Jewish authorities. Another interesting point was Pilate's presentation of Jesus to the public with his famous phrase "Ecce Homo!" This is usually translated as "Behold the Man", but that has never been exactly correct. The meaning of "homo" in its strict sense is "Human being", "person". Thus the saying really signified "Look! He is human!" In other words, "See, this is not God, but a bleeding and battered human being. How much more am I supposed to make him suffer?" Despite insistence by the Jewish leaders that Jesus be executed as a common criminal only, some of the crowd present shouted the traditional wording of "His blood be upon us and our people," meaning they were prepared to accept a sacrifice if civil capital punishment could be considered a valid method of offering a victim. As an educated man, Pilate would have been quite familiar with old procedures of pagan Sacred King practice. He was said to have been born in Britain, where it still took place unofficially. So his unique acknowledgement of ancient customs by the INRI inscription could well be construed as a concession to the undercurrent of basic beliefs held by most common people of that period. Those who wanted a sacred sacrifice could have it, and those demanding a political execution would have to be satisfied with the death sentence. Pilate was prepared to play it either way.

As history happened, Jesus was elected as a Sacred King among the anti-establishment elements of the post-crucifixion times, and so he became Liberator figure for those feeling oppressed, frustrated, ignored, or otherwise abused by the governing parties in power. These people and their supporters found the martyrdom of Jesus an ideal rallying point round which to raise their ideas of franchise and human hopes. So Jesus really became a Sacred King by adoption, after his death. It may not have been the standard way of working the tradition, but it was a welcome innovation, and a common King for the common people of many countries was certainly an uncommon concept in those days. If a Sacred King sacrifice was rejected by his own people, anybody at all could claim him. That was an old rule very rarely applicable. In the case of Jesus, his rejection by the Jewish priesthood and rulership simply offered him to the rest of hte world at large. Whether or not he has been accepted as he would have wished is still a debatable issue. At all events, the spirit of his sacrifice remains very much alive in our times.

There is no doubt that Jesus intended himself as a sacrifice on behalf of his own circle and those affiliating with them. In his own words he spoke of his blood being shed "for you and for many in remission of sins." Not for everyone evermore, be it noted, simply for those concerned just as other Sacred Kings had always done. In passing, it should be mentioned that in its translation of the Latin Mass into English, the Roman church has deliberately altered those words to read ". . for you and for all men so that sins may be forgiven." Perhaps it is best not to comment here on the obvious deviance with original meaning. In any case, "remission" does not mean actual forgiveness, but a lessening, merely an improvement of conditions.

What is especially interesting with the sacrifice of Jesus is that he was offering himself according to the custom of an ancient folk-faith which was outmoded in his day. Sacred King sacrifices were still going on, of course, particularly in the West and North, throughout Europe and Britain. This was why Christianity caught on in those areas—Jesus was not doing anything new, but something very old indeed, which touched deeply at the roots of folk-belief.

From our present point of human history in the West we may look back along the Sacred King story from many viewpoints. Nevertheless it is an actual account of the inner roots from which we rose. It amounts to an inherent individualism strong enough to defy death in the quest of an immortal identity; a willingness to sacrifice a lesser incarnate state of life in favor of what is believed to be larger living as a spiritual being. Naturally this does not show up in such direct and definite terms within the consciousness of average people. Probably very few are actually aware of such an inner aim at all in any clear or concise way. Most people feel the need to be themselves, but their behavior because of this drive varies enormously. Since with this work we are mainly concerned with the magical connections of our Tradition over the centuries, it may be as well to take a quick look at some of the salient points linking us from early times to this era. We shall perceive a definite pattern marking the inner movements of our Tradition so that we may know best how to fit ourselves in with the drift of this tide as it carries us through our own period. The solitary purpose or justification for dealing with the past is to help us tackle our present in order to improve our future prospects. Those intending to relate themselves with our Tradition by magical methods had best bear that in mind while they study the trends of our current spiritual situation.

4. Looking Over the Line

The dividing line between magic and religion in the West has always been very narrow. Therefore the history of one is often extremely difficult to distinguish from the other, especially in earliest days.

The attitude of Westernizing man towards magic was chiefly that it offered a means of extending his existence beyond limitation and into the unknown. If he ever reached the absolute edges of his current inner capacity, it seemed that nothing but sheer magic could enable him to push past that point and get a fresh grip on life in unfamiliar and hitherto secret surroundings. Now this is something very few humans enjoy doing. Most people like living well away from the edges of their experience, and are only driven thereto by crisis or some other major motivation. Religion generally tends towards making a background of belief against which we can arrange our lives to suit social and conventional requirements. Magic, on the other hand, pushes us past those beliefs into unfamiliar inner areas apt to be both alarming and unexpected. So when it came to making relationships with inner realities, the average Westerner preferred ready-made religion, but liked to have one or two magical tricks up his sleeve for emergencies. He still does.

The type of magic practiced by Western, pre-Christian man was something of a mixture between modern commando training and transcendental meditation. It worked on the assumption that a physical body had to be pushed to its limit and a mind moved to the end of its ability before anything really spiritual could be approached and bargained with. What this amounted to was a primitive but effective system of "forcing oneself" towards a state of threshold consciousness. Humans had learned that, when pressed to the very extremities of existence, a sort of "superstate" became momentarily reachable. In this state, an awareness of far more advanced beings was possible to some degree. It was feasible to form relationships with those by two main methods: religion, which tried to bring spiritual states close to ordinary human levels, and magic, which made humans look for what they sought on higher levels of encounter beyond normal reach.

It was scarcely surprising that magic as a way of life appealed to very few people in the Western world. Everybody practiced occasional items of magic, but it was left to the rare and dedicated devotee to take it up as a life-study. Such souls were extremely individualists. It may well be that a whole incarnation so spent added but the most minute fraction to the Tradition itself. More likely, it merely increased the depth of what was already there by the smallest amount imaginable. Nevertheless, each single effort made its metaphysical mark indelibly upon the continuum of our collective consciousness as Westerners.

The dominant theme of sacrifice from the old Sacred King formula continued to determine the shape of both religious and magical practices. Whoever intended to succeed as a priest or magician must be prepared to sacrifice something of himself to the "Divine" in exchange for what was wanted. Naturally, there were conflicts of opinion on this point. Some supposed a sacrifice of worldly wealth to be sufficient. Others sacrificed human companionship and spent lives of voluntary solitude in remote retreats. Some sacrificed their sex organs or blinded themselves in hopes of improved inner sight. Nastier types could be convinced that unwilling sacrifices of animals or other humans were acceptable substitutes. Black magic is common to all Traditions, unhappily, being a matter of motivation and method. It is doubtful if many magicians in those early days had very advanced and altruistic ideas of sacrificing their own lower natures to the Divine

Principle within themselves. The probability is that most of them worked on quid pro quo notions more in the nature of "If I give up this and this, then I expect my Gods to give me that and that in return." Elderly and exhausted magicians must have spent many sleepless nights wondering why their demands had never been met by the ungrateful Gods.

A Tradition, however, is built out of failures as much as successes, possibly more so. What matters is the effort and experience more than results. Strange and lonely figures of our past lived unrecorded incarnations apart from their contemporaries with apparently little or no effect on earth. They certainly published nothing, and spoke little to perhaps very few people. The legacy they left our world seemed nothing but their bones. Yet the contributions made by their consciousness to the Tradition they were following have helped keep it alive right down to our present day. Though unknown to us they were not unheard of by their own generations, who started stories and rumors about them. These passed into folk-legend and fantasy, still traceable in handed down tales. That may not seem very much today, but is actually far more than might be supposed. We have to ask ourselves what is so important about any image or symbol that it continues to stir human consciousness centuries after its exact origins have faded into oblivion. We must also face the conclusion that nothing could so continue unless its significance was really vital in some way to our present condition of existence. Whatever speaks to us from our past at all, has still something of value to tell us now and for the future.

What actually did early Western magicians do during their earthly lives? Disregarding the alleged marvels, we can be reasonably certain they accomplished a number of very solid spiritual advances in their times which influenced our own. They demonstrated how applied disciplines extend the awareness of a dedicated human being in the direction of Divinity. They claimed, and some would say substantiated, the possibility of communication between human beings and higher intelligences. They showed, in some instances, how intentional intervention from higher levels could affect and influence our affairs of earth-life. They were the forerunners of psychiatrists, psychotherapists, and most other modern medical dealings in personal problems. They related physical pattern symbology with internal mental and psychic states. They also acted as observers of natural history and meteorology, collectors of arcane information, students of sub and supernormal phenomena, and almost any other branch of intelligence leading away from average human interests and mundane preoccupations.

Nowadays we think ourselves so clever and advanced as we wallow in the materializations of our vaunted "technology". Yes, very remarkable indeed, but *when and how did it start happening?* It began in the minds and souls of men and women living a very long time ago who planted its seeds in a genetic garden still growing invisibly around us. All any generation does is dig out of itself what has been previously put there by ancestral archetypes and implant fresh ideas for future finders. However, this "Great Work" is certainly done in collaboration with higher than human types of intelligent entities, whether we are actively aware of this or not.

It is a beloved fiction of occult writers that large schools, colleges, or consortiums of adept magicians existed in mysterious and remote mountainous regions from which they directed the lives of lesser mortals throughout the world. The substratum of truth here is that those seeking individuation, away from mass-level human mentality, found isolation at higher altitudes a help toward achieving their aims. In seeking their own self-perfection, they could scarcely avoid a feed-back into deep levels of common consciousness. However, no genuine practitioner of magic in its true sense would deliberately interfere with the wills of other mortals. Nor would they be likely to live in large communities of their own kind, since that would precipitate the very publicity they needed to avoid. Their living pattern might allow for small association, family-sized at most. Tradition proved that the maximum of twelve round zero was the largest practical grouping in any locality. This produced the solar pattern of signs round a central nucleus, or Cosmic Cross, somewhat on the lines of the old stone Circles. There were probably very few centralizations of even that size among Western magicians. The more likely figure would be three or four. When needed, mundane contacts could be kept between groupings by their most mobile members.

The overall picture altered as waves of Celtic colonists went Westward. With them went their hierarchic priesthood which mixed magic, religion and mysticism in varying amounts. These Druids, as they were called, were by no means always beneficent patriarchal figures concerned with their people's welfare. They were the ruling members of an autocratic priestly caste. Quite apart from any of their reputed magical powers, they wielded considerable political and cultural influence among their people, the effect of which eventually sifted down into our Tradition. What they undoubtedly did was to systematize a great deal of the tradition, giving it structure and sophistication.

Though the Druids insisted on the transmission of the "Hidden Tradition" by oral means alone, they were anything but illiterate men. Their "mouth to ear" method of imparting spiritual instruction was a time-honored system of "passing the Word" directly along a carefully chosen line of consciousness connecting successive generations of humanity. A Tradition received in this way through direct human contacts linked with Inner intelligence is far more "alive" than if handed down on paper or other mechanical means of making records. Had the Druids been Hebrews, they would have called their teachings "Qabalah", which signifies exactly this "person to person" system of handing on something too sacred for writing down. Thus, Druid-taught Tradition was indeed a highly individual affair on its inmost levels, and therefore very suitable for Westernizing initiates.

While exact origins of "Druidism" remain undocumented, all indications point to influences among them tracing to Hellenistic, Hebrew, and Hindu sources. What they themselves put forward, however, was essentially their own Celtic synthesis and simplification of the principles behind those older faiths. That is to say, they had selected specific keys and leading points from ancient creeds and codes, then interpreted these in a more modern and practical way for the needs of the Celtic people. This was certainly their main contribution to our Western Inner Tradition, and it made indelible marks in the shape of our philosophic and moral outlooks.

Naturally, the Druids came into contact and competition with the older men of magic associated with megalithic cultures, and undoubtedly there were clashes of ideas and personalities. There must also have been useful exchanges of experience and mutually beneficial friendships. We have to remember, however, that the Celts were a forceful, militant people, with a warrior chieftainship upheld by an organized priesthood. Eventually they achieved dominance in Europe and Britain, older cultures becoming overwhelmed and outpaced by these pushing, ambitious people.

Gradually the megalithic type of magician retreated into the background or was absorbed into a more modern milieu. Since Druids disapproved of Stone Circle cults, the ancient meeting places became more disused in favor of the "Sacred Grove" system preferred by this newer priesthood.

The Druids also seem to have disliked the Sacred King sacrifices as practiced among indigenous countrymen. Since human life itself was held very cheaply, their antipathy must have been based on other considerations. Probably they realized that to overcome a competitive culture, its central theme has to be eliminated somehow. Not even they could entirely obliterate such an age old custom among semi-hostile and resentful natives of their new territory so, like later Christians, they compromised and settled for human sacrifice in the shape of condemned criminals or war prisoners doomed to destruction anyway. Also like later Christians, they seemed to think burning alive was a suitable death for those who defied authority. Needless to say, the deliberate destruction of utterly unwilling victims who must have hated those who killed them had nothing whatsoever to do with Sacred King principles at all. It was a brutal blasphemy against everything intended, and the Druids knew this well. They also knew that human crowds enjoyed watching others suffer, and how quickly a large gathering could be got together by the rumor of public executions in the near future. Crowds could be talked to and maybe masses covinced of what their manipulators wanted.

One art the Druids had superb command of was oration. Together with their bard collegues to supply music and verse, they really swayed listeners round to their ways of thinking. It was a new and indeed a thrilling experience to partake of a Druid "preach-in". Dull minds began to open and unused intelligences awakened to instructions or information hitherto unavailable. The Druids taught in terse, simple terms with allegorical allusions and local phraseology. People listened in fascination and awe to those amazing men who moved multitudes with their tongues and gestures. Almost none of the old-time magicians could compete with this fantastic flow of language and oracular entertainment, to say nothing of the fringe benefits provided in the way of food, refreshment, and other Celtic forms of hospitality. How long it took the Druids to preach a populace into acquiescence is uncertain. They certainly never suppressed or supplanted the

"Old Religion" entirely, as evidence shows. Moreover, the Western Tradition is indebted to them for an impact of inner awakenings at a time when we really needed rousing from a rather torpid state of spiritual slumbering.

Druids made one very important contribution to the Western Tradition which few, if any, modern commentators realize. They offered an alternative "salvation system" to the hitherto unchallenged Sacred King convention. What the Druids preached was not unlike the fundamentalism of the Jewish faith, but included reincarnation. Not unlike the Jews, the Druids held to a "chosen people" or "sanctification of the elect" teaching. Only those souls who came up to pre-specified spiritual standards would make top grade in afterlife. There was little hope for the rest.

What the Druids did for the West was lay the foundation stones of alternative inner ways which later developed into Catholicism and Protestantism. The Catholics trace back to the older Sacred King beliefs, while the Protestants link with the newer Druidic form of faith. The major difference between the two was one of relationship of Man with God. The former believed in the principle of sacrifice effecting redemption, and the latter believed in direct individual applications to Divinity which might or might not find favor if the applicant followed out prescribed teachings faithfully. This last had a lot to recommend it for intensely individual Westerners with sufficient faith in themselves to take a high-risk gamble with God. Unhappily, we are still paying for the dissension and enmity which arose between these factions. It may yet be the work of magic among us to reconcile this rift in the future.

Hard on the Druids' heels advanced Roman Imperialism with its multi-religious military might. So far as Roman rulers were concerned, their adopted God-figures were synonymous with their own ambitions. If alien God-forms accepted this, well and good—if not, let the Legions loose to put them in their places. So long as Roman authority was acknowledged, let others worship or believe whatever they wanted. The general policy was to equate local gods with recognized Roman divine names, then charge their worshippers for associate membership in the God-club. No Roman goverment ever persecuted people for their religious beliefs purely and simply. The so-called anti-Christian persecutions were entirely political, because Christianity became a dangerous counterforce to the Roman establishment and way of life. Rome dealt with Druids drastically for the same reason. In the West, Druids were leading almost the entire resistance movement to Roman occupation and intrusion in Celtic dominated countries. So the Druids had to be smashed as an organized threat.

To break up an outer organization with political and military power is a calculable operation. To eradicate the inner effects such an organization may have made upon the minds and souls of a people is another affair entirely. Druids may have died in large numbers, but they stayed alive in the Tradition. Moreover, many of them, like the older magicians, simply faded into a camouflaged obscurity and continued as an "underground movement".

It is interesting to note that few of the imported sects and cults accompanying the Legions really appealed to Westerners. One exception, the Mithraic cult, happened to be a very exclusive all-male and mainly military membership. Its attraction for the West, despite its oriental origins, lay with its simple Good-over-Evil formula, blood sacrifice of a surrogate Bull-king, and graded system of promotion supposed to be connected with character tests to prove worthiness. However, its own exclusiveness almost automatically ended it as an active affair. Most Westerners stuck with their now rather run-down remains of "Old Religion" or clandestine cults among themselves which looked for new Light on perpetual problems.

The Western spiritual situation became one of ferment, anxiety, uncertainty, oppression, opportunism, and an altogether unsettled inner climate of a very tense nature. Who knew for sure what to believe any more? Old people said one thing, but the young were looking for another. If one God was as good as the next why bother with any of them? The only God claiming universal recognition was Money. Financial fingers were spreading fast just then, and currency coined in one country could be accepted in others at heavy discounts. Most of the Gods were beginning to take back seats before the victorious march of Mammon, the all-conqueror, and the Tradition of the West had begun to include a commercial code. Its inmost and more magical contents were retiring gracefully behind screens of legend linking the mysterious lands of memory with a world of wishful thinking. Those who knew what the Tradition was all about handed hints of it to whoever they trusted and passed on whatever they could to perhaps a very few that were able to accept and honor it in the same spirit. Peasants stolidly kept up customs they could not claim to understand but felt they ought to follow. Poets invented rhymes, riddles, and other symbols of consciousness which they prayed might pertain to a larger life they felt themselves part of. The People plodded along in pursuit of profit as usual, and so the Tradition went with them all in its own way, waiting for fresh energies to enlarge it.

It was at this time that Christianity began spreading Westward with surprising speed. It made little impression in the East among already established and organized faiths, but it went West as if it were something eagerly anticipated and expected. While it did not reach wide recognition immediately, it quickly sprang up in small quantities here and there especially in Britain and parts of Gaul. Moreover, there was an organized linkage between most of these little groupings. What was the secret of their phenomenal rise into positions of power with such relative swiftness?

Their real secret was that they were spearheading a sort of spiritual socialism promising equal chances of salvation for all mankind, including women, regardless of rank, wealth or status. It was a religion of revolution offering emancipation and the highest heavenly hopes to the poorest, meanest, and most abject members of the human race. All anyone had to do was to say the right words amounting to "Christ for King" and instant initiation happened. Everyone would be brothers and sisters in the Lord and paradise was only a few moments away for believers. Glory was at hand, and God loved whoever came into the Movement.

What we have to bear in mind in our times is that, all over the Western world, there were thousands and thousands of folk who had been steadily pressured into positions where a liberating message of that nature meant everything in life to them. They were mostly the ordinary people and especially what we would now call "workers" who had felt themselves helplessly outclassed, oppressed, and their pleas insultingly ignored by Gods and Governments alike. The Gods were deaf, the governments demanding, life was hard, and at the end of it what? Pain, poverty, and extinction! Heavens were for the wealthy, and the most others could hope for was servitude forever in an afterlife if they were fortunate to get that far. The various mystery cults had become more and more exclusive, insisting on higher admission fees, more stringent scrutiny of applicants. No hope for poor folk there. They could join throngs at the back of officially supported temples, but they always felt unwanted or unwelcomed by the paid priesthood and the elite membership. There just did not seem to be any spiritual opportunities specially available to them. They had advanced somewhat above Peasant level, so the old barely remembered rites had not much meaning for them. Yet, not having Poet abilities, they could make little meaning out of life for themselves. They were getting more and more out of inner touch with their Tradition and becoming bitter, disillusioned, helpless, and very disheartened people losing what is most valuable in anyone's life—their sense of inherited destiny.

All of a sudden an amazing message ran among them like wildfire. Their souls had been liberated at last. A God had come to earth again and freed everyone of them by sacrificing his human life as a Sacred King should. At last, the days of oppressors and tyrants were numbered. A heavenly world was at hand where there would be no poor, sick, or unhappy people any more. The wicked exploiters would be sent to Hell forever, and everybody else would be so happy together they would scarcely know what to do with themselves. Everything they had ever wanted would be available for the asking, and there would be no work, worry, weeping or weariness ever again. The day of mankind's dearest dream was here at last. Equality, Liberty, and Brotherhood had arrived in earnest.

Christianity would never have caught on in the West as it did if the people had not instinctively identified it with their old magical religion and the Sacred King. Under Roman law and with officially established religions of that time, human sacrifice to Gods was illegal and animals had been substituted. However irreligious or indifferent folk had become, they still held traces of an ineradicable Tradition in themselves which told them that much of their troubles was due to forsaking the Old Ones and following foreign customs. Now one of those Old Ones had come to claim them again in a far wider sense than ever before. A radical note was rung that was heard with crystal clarity all round the Western world. We should remember that the origins of

Christianity were Mediterranean, and so were the beginnings of the megalithic cultures. It was a family faith returning to home ground again, this time in a modern manner.

Soon enough all the symbology of Sacred Kingship surrounded the faraway figure of a Man-God who had died for anyone willing to accept his saviorship. Every time his sacrifice was symbolized by the bread and wine substitutes for flesh and blood his spirit would be with worshippers, as simply as that. This revolutionary idea suited the mood of people themselves, and the new faith was to become a symbol of resistance against oppressive establishments and resented authorities. Sympathetic members of the older Mystery cults joined up bringing information and ideas they had sworn to hold secret. Even some old-time magical practitioners came to help revive what they hoped was a restoration of their beloved beliefs. There emerged a full-time priesthood preaching the doctrines which would later lead to the downfall of Rome as an empire, and its future establishment as a religious center.

II.

With the coming of Christianity, the idea of individualized Sacred Kingship entered and became part of the Western Tradition. Such a supreme privilege had always been for selected heroes alone, and these were exclusively masculine. Now it became accepted that something of the semi-divine nature was imparted to every soul opening itself to the Christ-Spirit, including women. Even the worst of sinners had hopes of redemption once the right words were said. Whatever the faults and fallibilities of early Christianity, it certainly brought hope, comfort, and a great deal of helpful inspiration to large numbers of deprived and despairing people. It gave them something to really care about, and they felt truly cared for in return. They knew that somehow they were altering history as they believed for the better. Whether they realized it or not, they were also defining and changing the character of the Western Inner Tradition.

Naturally there was opposition to the Christian movement. It was a threat to Government, a menace to the set ways of contemporary society, a dangerous and subversive sect that stated slaves and masters were spiritual equals. It upset young people's minds and old people's convictions. Repressive rules were enforced against them but they still florished. Persecution proved inadequate. In the end, an exasperated establishment found only one practical course—buy into the movement at top level and steadily take over its organization. It took a very long time and was only marginally successful. Many were the rebels and malcontents being labelled as heretics and revolutionaries. Once more the "Us-and-Them" war went on while secret Traditiona-lists went underground with the speed and ease of veteran evaders. But, not before they had left a whole series of symbols in the churches interpretable by anyone attaining a certain aware-ness of the Tradition itself.

At the very far West of the world which was then Britain, an interesting mixture of cultures was beginning to build up. Roman strength may have officially broken Druid dominance, but many of them had merely turned their labels round and written "Christian priest" or something else on the other side. By this time, a Celtic Christian church had come into existence as an almost independent organization which managed to maintain co-existence with other indigenous faiths. Its magic came from the priest-kings, its philosophy and preaching from the Druids, and its mysticism from initiates of the secret systems.

How far the Celtic church would have evolved its own interpretation of Christianity over the ages can only be guessed. Its culture was not acceptable to the tough and primitive type of pagan who preferred older and cruder ways of living. Nor was its independent outlook acceptable to the central controlling caucus then reaching out from Rome. A well-financed and backed mission headed by Augustine in England established a strong bridgehead for Roman dominance of official religion in the West. Christianity, which had once been so many people's hopes of spiritual freedom, was now becoming owned and directed by those with wealth and power.

It is probably about this period that the magical way into the Western Tradition became more or less consolidated. Hitherto it had associated very closely with religion, but now official religion was repudiating its magical connections with increasing vehe-mence. The gap was widening very fast, and decisions of preference and loyalties had to be made. Standards of education were improving slowly, and contacts could be kept up among literate circles by writing, even if this meant using a coded symbolism for the sake of security. Once magic of any sort had been labelled anti-Christian and incurred the antipathy of authorities, the obvious course to take was one of silence, secrecy, and caution in all such affairs.

Magic was taking on a new meaning among Traditionalists. It stood for independence of inner opinion and individual association with spiritual contacts made by methods not to be found in prayer-books or proceedings of parliament. Collectively, it meant clandestine contact among like-minded specialists. This was about the time when the Poet and Peasant streams of our Tradition parted company so widely in apparently opposite directions. The division was mainly one of economy and status. The poor Peasant clung to his soil-level culture with whatever he could remember of the Old Religions customs, by now debased and distorted almost out of recognition. The Poet, patronized by a wealthier clientele, raised the ideology of the Tradition to the greatest heights reachable at that period. There was naturally a wide diversion between the two cultural extremities and communication between them became more and more difficult.

The Peasant end of the Tradition relied on its natural taciturnity and suspicion of strangers to preserve what privacy it could concerning its carried-on customs. Ecclesiastics raged away at paganism running rampant, but the peasants stolidly let the sermons roll past and went their own way behind the bishops' backs. The Poet, on the other hand, inspired with imagination, invented all kinds of security systems for ensuring secrecy and integrity among adherents to the more intellectual and mystical end of the Tradition. Allegories, allusions, in-talk, codes, recognition procedures, and all the elaborate and fascinating cover-ups still in use among some occultists today, were set up as camouflage for a growing fraternity of Western Inner Traditionalists. While admittedly essential in one respect, it gave rise to all kinds of misinterpretations. A major difficulty with complicated procedural technicalities is that people become so involved with them, they often miss the vital truths those trivia were employed to safeguard.

Although withdrawn beneath the surface of external Western living, the Inner Tradition continued to show traces of itself amongst the people and in the churches. Somehow, the old Mother-Goddess made her demure come-back under the mask of Mary, and pre-Christian deities reappeared as saints such as Bride (Brigit) and Dennis (Dionysius). The major religious festival of Easter took its name from a pagan Spring goddess. Celts still used the Solar Cross, local craftsmen carved ancient emblems and faces into ecclesiastical ornamentation—wherever anyone looked, signs of barely submerged beliefs could be seen by appreciative eyes. The Christian Church, which began by challenging the supremacy of stultified spiritual leadership, was now on the receiving end of many resistance movements against its own authoritarianism.

By this time, the behavior pattern of the Western Inner Tradition was quite evident. At its foundation, the spiritual basis of the Tradition was rooted in individuation through initiation along accepted lines of Light-Life. The effects of this energy impelled people incarnating into the Western world to arrange their lives in some accordance with its influence. As might be expected, this went very wide of its central aim. Therefore once an established drift away from that metaphysical mark carried Western culture and civilization past a certain point, an automatic counter-current arose to correct this. Our history shows that over the centuries we have been swinging from side to side over the centerline of our Inner Tradition.

The real work of initiates of the Western Way consists chiefly of keeping conscious touch with this precise spiritual stream running through our Tradition, so that agencies are available in this world to make constant course-correction possible. It is not what those Initiates do which makes that difference, but what they actually *are* in themselves. Applied energy from inner sources passing through the focal points they provide will actually *do* whatever is necessary. The Initiates themselves simply have to *be* what, where, and when they are in order for such forces to operate through them.

Perhaps the most subtle and sophisticated Traditionalist opposition to orthodox Christian dominance was, and to some degree still is, the legendary quest of the Holy Grail. Cast into conventional Christian mysticism, the Grail story is ostensibly centralized on the Cup of the Last Supper, and various heroic activities in connection with attaining access to it. The hidden story is that of the old Sacred King sacrifice and the necessity for its restoration in a workable way among the elite of Western evolution. Using the British Celtic chieftain Arthur and contemporary figures associated with him as dramatis personae, the Grail Legend retold the romance of the ancient Priest-Kings in heavily veiled allegory, and pleaded for re-institution of the system among those entitled to its inheritance by birth or belief.

The "Holy Grail" is actually the Sang Real, or Blood Royal. This refers to the King whose blood must be shed on behalf of his people, and also his true line of descent from Sacred King stock. The "Knights of the Grail" were a select circle of suitable surrogates, from among whose number one had to be chosen by design or lot as a voluntary victim. That was the dreaded "Grail Question" which had to be answered if ill were to be averted. The famous Round Table was an idealistic form of the Stone Circles where Sacred Kings were once selected from an assembled company. All the ancient symbology was resurrected and strung together in a new and exciting form. Exciting, because it aroused ancestral and genetic awareness in whoever instinctively felt its secret significance. New, because it brought back our oldest ways of worship adapted for humans who had advanced to higher arcs of consciousness over the centuries.

With the advent of the Grail mysteries, our Western Tradition made a spiritual stride of immense significance. It was as though the awakening spirit of the West were getting a fresh grip on life. Our days of childish confidence in "Divine Goodness" saving us from the effects of our follies had ended at last, and a more adult outlook had arisen. There was an acknowledgement that those who wanted salvation had better fight for it on their own rather than rely on providential rescue programs.

The implications of the Grail cult were that the Christian Church as it stood did not represent the full redemption scheme for mankind. There were certain secrets withheld from it which only an initiated elect could comprehend. Those, of course, were the death and re-birth formulas of the old Sacred King system. There was also the orally transmitted idea of a blood line in Britain directly descended from Jesus himself. The covering symbolism for this notion was that Joseph of Aramithea retired to Avalon or Glastonbury in Somerset, Britain, bearing with him the "Holy Grail" and two vessels containing the blood and sweat of the crucified Jesus. The "two vessels" were said to be living people. One, Mary the mother of Jesus, was the "blood", the other was her grandson or the "seed" of Jesus, sweat being an euphemism for seminal fluid. There is nothing known with the slightest certainty concerning the truth of such a rumor. Beyond the bare possibility itself, nothing survives for sure. Various "Keepers of the Grail" were supposed to have the secret handed down from one generation to another, but eventually the "Grail" was reputed to have removed altogether from this world to a mysterious place called "Sarras". Whether this meant the direct line had died out or a less literal interpretation should apply is a matter for speculation.

Those who grasped something of what the Grail meant started their own searchings and strivings along the inner lines its symbolic story suggested. Perhaps the concept which the Grail-idea put most into people's minds was that of a "Panacea" or Universal Remedy for all that could ever go wrong in life. Obtain the Grail—whatever that was—and evils would end for the attainer absolutely. The Grail provided the power to solve every spiritual problem mankind would ever have. A little later this concept came out on a somewhat lower scale as the "Stone" of the Alchemists.

Although we have not yet discovered a Panacea for all our problems, the concept itself is of enormous importance within the Tradition. Whatever the mind of man can concieve will eventually evolve. The process may take thousands of years and more, yet with time and work we can manifest what comes into our consciousness. It is the initial idea which is so vital. So our Grail-Panacea is yet to come in a finalized form if we follow the lines it established in our Tradition only a few centuries ago. It only remains for us to go inside and get it for ourselves.

The Grail-concept was virtually the last really great reappearance of the Sacred King theme among Western Traditionalists. From thence on they seem to have been more concerned with the philosophical and scientific side of its nature. This is because of slow but steady increases of intellect among a far wider section of Western humans. Earlier generations responded to problems more naturally by emotions and feeling. Later, an awakening awareness of calculable and controllable inner intelligence demanded a far more deliberate and careful approach to our supra-mundane affairs. This appeared very clearly during the next three almost simultaneous stages of alteration which adapted our Tradition to medieval living.

From the purely philosophical angle, the most significant was the adoption of the body of spiritual symbolism known as the Qabalah, or "oral teaching." Synods of scholars were sifting, synthesising, and collating all such ancient knowledge and experience into condensed formularies which, it was hoped, would carry a whole inheritance of enlightenment into the future. Today we should say they were computerizing it down to basic tapes. Eventually they cast the entirety of their conscious capacity into the design of the Tree of Life. The tree was a plan of perfection utilizing an ideal proportional relationship between the primal principles of Life as an expression of Divine and human existence. As a "salvation symbol" it has yet no equal, except possibly the Cosmic Cross.

Because of its arcane arrangement and abstruse presentation, the Hebrew version of the Inner Tradition remained relatively unknown and unappreciated except in very small circles. Today it is one of the principal pillars of Western Inner practice and belief. Many suppose it to be entirely of Jewish origin, but this is not so. In the eyes of orthodox Judaism, Qabalah is heretical. Especially since it acknowledges a feminine principle in the Deity, and incorporates ideas familiar to the Old Religion.

The sublime idea behind this contribution to expanding Western consciousness was roughly this: incorporate esoteric experience into a single set of keys. These could then be used as permanent paths for anyone seeking to unlock the spiritual secrets of their own unexplored inner beings. In other words, try and arrange everything so that once the "Key-ideas" were properly grasped, they would automatically open up whole chains of consciousness and awareness. Then make a "Master-Key" pattern that would work the whole scheme successfully. Such a Master-Key is the Tree of Life, now becoming much more widely known in the West, though still only likely to have appeal for intellectual eclectics.

Of far wider interest, due to sheer human avarice and ambition, was Alchemy, though this is more or less marginal to the Tradition. Its ostensible aim, of course, was an infallible cure for the wrongs of poverty, ill-health, and other horrors of humanity. At least out of Alchemy emerged most of the chemical know-how which set the West ahead of others in this world for a long time. We still have Alchemy with us in one way, represented by the persistent belief that money is the answer to everything on earth, and given sufficient gold anything at all is possible. The modern fashionable name for that Stone is "socio-economics". On higher levels yet, Alchemy still says that if only the worst and weakest side of human nature could be transmuted into something really shining and splendid, we need not live on these low levels any longer but could transcend them altogether and exist as much better kinds of beings. All we yet have to find is the "Magic Stone" making this possible.

Another tangent from our Tradition which is having its impact on our present living was the Rosy Cross formula of philosophy, romantic religion, and humanitarianism. In its early days, this could almost be described in present terms as "pop-occultism". It coincided with the currents of religious reformation and the spirit of renaissance which at long last was sweeping through the Western world.

The Rosicrucian formulary caught the imagination of intelligent and progressive people of that period much as the Grail concept had stirred their forbears, but from a somewhat different angle. Wrapped up in pleasantly romantic language was a spiritual and social code of conduct acceptable to average mortals who genuinely wanted their world to become a better place for people. Its appeal was and yet is sane and sensible ways of working and thinking, sound spiritual standards, and what is generally thought of as good, ethical behavior.

We have to remember the climate of the times during which the Rosy Cross concept made its appearance. Corruption in Church and political practice was so commonplace that few seriously believed it could be altered except by smashing the system and trying to build a better one. Here and there, some were trying to form tangents along new lines that would lead away from the mess into less contaminated inner areas. The Rose-Cross scheme was one of these. It said in effect "Have courage. Pick up your own paths and simply walk quietly out of this man-made muddle by yourself. You have Light in yourself which will infallibly lead you if you follow its rays. Never mind anything that Church, State, or other confusers of consciousness tell you."

Like the Grail, the Rosy Cross appealed to an elite that instinctively understood its import, but this time it was among a much wider range of society. The only qualification was comprehension and willingness to work for specified social and spiritual aims. Although the visionary nucleus of the fabled Order was a college of one hundred full members the theory was that if only a hundred entirely upright people could be found to form a complete circle of spiritual integrity, the effects from such an inner stronghold could multiply and magnify enough to influence everyone else for the better in time. It was the ten just men needed to save Sodom and Gomorrah all over again, except that increased population called for more saviors.

Much has and can still be made of the Rose Cross symbol. The Rose is to the West as the Lotus is to the East: the flowering of the ethnic spirit in a balanced state of beauty and perfection. It was also the symbol of resurrection, thus reviving a very old contract with Cosmos—the Sacred Kingship ideal. A red rose is symbolic of passion in the sense of deep and true feeling. The Sacred King sacrifice in Christian mythology is called the "Passion" of Jesus. Used in context with a Cross, the Rose was to show what amounted to a "new Christianity" for Western people, exemplifying a spirit of self-sacrifice for the sake of attaining a state of perfection among people. The emblem was to be a badge for those intending to incarnate a Christ-spirit into themselves in order to help other humans around them. It was the best of Old and New combined into concepts meant for carrying folk forward to the future with hopes of peace and perfection.

The reformation which went on in the "Hidden Church" as well as in the realms of official religion spread over an increasingly wide front. Much of the organization and procedures still used in "Lodges" or "Temples" of present day occultism were formulated about that period. However, the most interesting projection was that which became known as "Masonry."

Trade guilds incorporating mutual benefit schemes for sickness, unemployment, hardship, and burial contingencies had been going for a very long time one way or another. In old days they had usually been associated with specific Temples, cults, or denominational backgrounds with which membership in good standing was obligatory. The Christian Church took over the running of these from earlier pagan hands, and in Europe and Britain they were chiefly controlled by an orthodox ownership. With the advent of "New Christianity", however, the situation began to change, inclining towards "humanism" rather than "religiousness". It was beginning to matter less that a man belonged to any particular branch of religion, and more that he was a worthwhile fellow being. If he came within certain standards of uprightness and ability, then he was worth admitting into similar circles for his own sake. If not, then let him wait outside where he belonged.

It was principally into the "closed shop" gatherings or "Lodges" of the Stoneworkers or Masons that ideas originating from "New Magic" infiltrated and found fruitful roots. This is interesting when one remembers it was among the old Stone Circle constructors that Western forms of magic really began. The formation and working principles of guild lodges having an elected officership and selected membership had existed for a long while. Before men could qualify for better positions of pay or privilege, they had to pass standard tests to prove their fitness, which everyone admitted was perfectly fair. Over the centuries they had evolved their own customs and conventions in connection with their craft. There wasn't really much magical about all that.

Where the magic came in was through a systematic alignment and association of the common tools and terms of their trade with specific spiritual equivalents. The mundane items used in the manufacture of material structures were slanted symbolically so as to constantly direct their attention toward higher realms of reality. While accomplishing the least work in this world, they were automatically reminded of life on more exalted levels. They were trained to find spiritual significance in every single earthly act they did, and alter the monkish precept "Work *and* Pray" into "Work *is* Prayer."

Eventually, of course, groups of non-laboring men began setting up their own social gatherings on much the same scale, retaining symbolism from the stoneworkers' impedimenta and procedures, but accepting it on entirely figurative lines. They became, specifically, Free-Masons. Those wishing to work in other ways adopted their favorite systems of symbolism, but usually formed their organizations according to very similar schemes. Hence the apparent connection between some of the so-called "Occult Orders" and orthodox Freemasonry. One particularly useful function those groups served was providing a place for the Peasants, Poets, and People of our joint Inner Tradition to meet and sort out problems for future solution together.

If we look back to Europe about the first Rosicrucian period, we find that a lot of the Peasants, some of the People, and a few of the Poets were not doing well at all. Church-State persecutions were in full swing against dissention from official faiths. Caught between the two-pronged fork of heresy and witchcraft, endless folk met agonizing ends at the hands of holy hypocrisy. Even today there is considerable misunderstanding about this situation, so a few vital points may as well be clarified.

In the first place, nobody was executed for being a non-Christian of any kind. A heretic could only be a member of the Church, who denied official doctrine. Jews, Muslims, Hindus, etc., being classed as heathen, could not be heretics. None but baptised Christians who abjured whatever they were told to believe by authorities could therefore be classed as heretics. No matter what other opinions they held of Christian doctrine, if those did not agree with the laid down formulas, then heresy was taken for granted and dealt with accordingly.

Witchcraft was different altogether. That was specifically a deliberate working of evil against God and man alike by means of what were termed "diabolic arts". Those could be anything from ill-wishing to poisoning, but the implication was that "evil spirits" were involved in the deal to make any act one of witchcraft. For instance, to curse anyone personally was against rules of religion, or to poison them was murder and against all laws. Had the curse been in the name of the Devil, or the poison supposedly suggested or supplied by a diabolical agency, then that was witchcraft. Only intervention by anti-human intelligences constituted the Church variety of witchcraft, which of course carried the death sentence.

In order to make their charges stick, the Church had to invent Satanism and accuse any odd pagans they picked up of working witchcraft and worshipping Satan. Witchcraft on the statute books was a crime applicable to anybody whatever, be they Christians, Jews, or nothing in particular. It was an offence *per se* and punishable on its merits alone.

Once the Church and State got into its drive against any surviving remnants of paganism in Europe, those who were still trying to keep up age-old and mostly forgotten formula of ancient nature faiths either had to cover up fast or risk ruin. Their primitive and often brutal practices, acceptable among themselves, were declared works of witchcraft or, worse still, Satanism, by the Church. Satan meant nothing at all to the primitives, except some spirit the Christians were afraid of for their own reasons. The lower-level inheritors of the Sacred King system had never heard of a "Black Mass". It was the Church authorities who supposed any sacrifice of life outside those they permitted themselves had to be an illegal offering to the Devil. So the Black Mass of the Satanists was, strictly speaking, originated by Christians. So was witchcraft, though some now suppose it to be a survival of paganity. Pagans were no more witches than anyone else in any era. The word means etymologically a worker of wickedness, and was applied to pagans by the Church, not themselves. Only under torture would they admit to any rubbish suggested by inquisitors.

There is no doubt that, in many instances, pagan practice in Europe had degenereated badly. With fewer and fewer responsible and initiated individuals to control and guide them, the Peasants who still clung to paganism were sometimes indulging in vicious sexual and sadistic behavior as releases from their oppressions. That, however, does not justify the brutality and sadism of those authorities in tackling the situation. What is more, it made a bad connection with our Tradition which is showing up very strongly in our times all these years later. It also lost us valuable links with ancient lines which will take quite a while to catch up with. Perhaps worst of all, it produced a systematic religion of Evil which flourishes yet and forms a focus for anti-human agencies.

Despite its despotism, the Church was fighting a losing battle against an awakening inner awareness among Western people which was stirring their souls into activity. Visions of a far future we have not yet reached were reflected from the mirrors of the past, perceived only partially at that period, and projected into all sorts of schemes and stratagems which sound absurd to us today. Whether they were really any sillier than we remains to be seen in other incarnations.

It is difficult to imagine a more muddled mess than the magic of the middle ages. This was indeed a hotch-potch of fragments from every part of the Tradition jumbled together into the most extraordinary junk-heap of collected curiosa likely to be met on literary levels. Its basic idea was bullying demons into doing whatever dirty work was wanted, such as getting rich quickly, killing enemies, grabbing girls, or generally gratifying whichever desire came topmost at any moment. There were two ways of doing this. One was to make friends with powerful angels who could command the demons to obey human orders. That was "White" magic. The other was offering one's own soul to the Spirit of Evil in exchange for a few years of every possible earthly enjoyment. "Black" magic.

Maybe the motivation behind it all is the most interesting part of it. First, there is the implicit admission of those concerned that they are utterly unable to obtain anything they want by their own abilities or resources. Then is their somewhat ambiguous appeal to the good nature of one class of spirit that those will command the bad nature of another type to work for a human being demanding something that neither species of spirit is particularly interested in. It does sound childishly like saying "Dear God, please make the Devil give me something You won't." Much of medieval magic was an active expression of anti-clericalism and defiance of authority. If the Devil was against the Church and State, then Hail, Devil, here we come, magic and all. Moreover, since all so-called magical practices were prohibited by the Church, they afforded a most luxurious sense of secret sin to practitioners.

On the whole, medieval magic as described in its text books contributed little that was worthwhile to our Tradition. In addition, it left a legacy of conflicting and confusing ideas which have not yet been properly cleared up. There is one particularly brilliant exception which stands out with the brightness of a beacon against a background of gloom. This was the "Abramelim system" attributed to a Hebrew source, but far more likely to have come from the same school which produced the Rose-Cross and similar systems of practical spiritual philosophy. This outstanding work, if correctly appreciated and applied, has as much, if not more, significance in our times as it ever had originally.

What the Abremelim system amounts to is a psychological process of individuation conducted as an assualt on the citadel of inner consciousness. It was calculated to achieve a state of awareness between one's ordinary waking conditions and the deeply dormant "higher self" not normally in close contact with mundane levels of living. If all the directions and provisos were faithfully fulfilled then the system could indeed make this possible to a recognizable degree. The point arose, however, that only very exceptional souls would be able to work it, which was no help at all for more ordinary mortals. Nevertheless, after considerable adaption and modification, it is derivations of the Abremelim system which have become integral parts of modern training programs among most reputably sponsored schools of initiation.

A major medieval addition to our magical Tradition was the Tarot pack of oracular cards. They became to the West what the I Ching is to the East, sort of universal advisory. Based on the four main magical instruments, twenty-two special Symbols, and suits of four court cards and ten numerals, it cannot be coincidence that these align with the Tree of Life and its significance. The cards, like the Tree, give coverage to all situations humans are likely to encounter in the course of living. No one seems to know exactly how they derived from previous packs. Some indications point to the south of France, linking occult movements of that time such as Qabbalism, Catharism, the Troubadours, Templars, and others. Many guesses have been made at the meaning of the term "Tarot". Perhaps the most likely theory traces to two Hebrew roots. ThAR—to mark, grave, or delineate, and OTh, at the time, presently, soon. In other words, something to determine or mark what will happen. They are certainly still used for that purpose and their popularity is yet increasing.

The esoteric significance of the Tarots is chiefly that they codify very cleverly the whole way of working with our Inner Tradition. They were said to have been expressly designed so that, concealed as a set of cards in common use, all the fundamentals of our Tradition could be reconstructed in any century by whoever realized what was involved. It is maybe significant that the Tarots made an appearance on the European scene at about the era when the Church was consolidating its power prior to making its maximum push against all disagreeing with its dogmas or dictatorial status. They certainly spread among all classes of people quite rapidly as a method of amusement and gambling, which was probably what their originators hoped. Providing the symbols simply kept circulating around the general consciousness of ordinary Westerners, the inner truths of our Tradition would not be lost to future generations.

That makes the modern concern with Tarots, mostly among our younger folk, very interesting indeed. Whether they realize instinctively that they are looking for and also at the root-meaning of their Western Inner Tradition may be a little uncertain, but what really matters is they continue looking. The more they look the more they will asssuredly find. They may think they are looking for their personal futures, and so indeed they are, because the future of their Tradition is theirs as well. The keys to the Tarots do not lie in their actual design so much as in their fundamental meanings. Designs may be altered so easily, but basic principles have to remain intact. However, if anyone is seeking for secrets in detailed Tarot designs, they had best work with the Waite pack and study these carefully with a good magnifying glass. If an original pack can be used, so much the better, because some of the essential details did not transfer well to newer reprints.

Leaping the odd century or so towards our times we will pause briefly to glance at an odd, old figure bent over neat lists of tabulations. He wonders if his long life was worth while, and why his spirit friends should have left him to a cold, lonely, and almost penniless old age. He is Dr. John Dee, mathematician, astrologer, intelligence agent, alchemist, and spiritualist. How much the money would have meant to him then, which people are now paying for books about him! Himself a victim of confidence tricks, popular prejudice, and misfortune, what had he to leave our Tradition?

Dee seems mostly remembered for one idea alone: that it might be possible to speak with discarnate entities, providing a mutually acceptable verbal symbolism was used. Dee himself believed that with the aid of his medium, Kelly, he had invented such a code, which he named the Enochian language because Enoch was supposed to talk directly with God and the angels. Being a cryptographer, Dee was convinced that intelligence of any kind could be reduced to sonic or visual symbolism translatable in equal terms on all levels of its application. If this were so, then non-human entities could codify a communication, send this through a connecting channel to be received by humans who would then decode into whatever language they spoke and grasp the significance of a heavenly message in their own speech.

It is the principle behind this idea which is of value in our Tradition, rather than poor Dee's attempts at it in his day. Nowadays, we are concerned with finding a common code of consciousness throughout Cosmos itself, and that sort of speech is more likely to be comprehended by computers than human brains. Yet the concept remains that we should be able to communicate with other orders of living intelligence if only we had mutual terms of translation. Symbologists have been seeking this for centuries with only partial success.

Skipping lightly back a little ahead of Dr. Dee, we strike a particularly turbulent period. Persecutions for witchcraft at some points are matched by utter denials of it at others, Church and dissenters detesting each other's doctrines, and controversy in all directions leading to clarification in none. It is a characteristic of the Western Way that if spiritual situations become stalemates unalterable by compromise, then conflict is often chosen as an escape from the impasse. The Civil War in England altered the attitudes of people towards Church and Dissenters alike, devaluing them both as betrayers of beliefs they tried to prove by persecution and prejudice. Between their battles, they turned many minds away from reliance on religion in any form and set them seeking fresh beliefs that did not depend on dogmas or dictatorship at all.

This point marked the coming forward of what looked like a new faith acknowledging no Deity except the exploring spirit within Mankind. Philosophy was producing science as we now see it. This did not so much deny every old God-Figure as proclaim its "declaration of independence" from all of them.

Humans were waking up to a realization that the wonderful Heaven they had been promised as a reward for sufferings on earth was a very uncertain speculation to say the least. Nor did increasingly intelligent beings find a prospect of eternal euphoria an attractive proposition. Given a choice, they would far rather continue progressing quietly and effectively along their lines of evolution. In any case, if a problematical Heaven was to be filled with the unpleasant sectaries and sanctimonious of earth, it would scarcely be worth entering anyway. It would be far better to find some other way, even if it ended in nothing. Better to believe in No-God, rather than any who ruled human lives with such ruthlessness. So did scientific scepticism speak as the "Age of Reason" rose from the depth of our Tradition to provide pathways for followers disgusted with "Divine dipensations."

From this point on, the Tradition offered three main threads into its depths. The Sacred King lead exemplified in Christianity whether Anglo-, Roman, or otherwise. The Independent lead exemplified by Dissenters and other Deists. Lastly, the Scientific lead for those that rejected religion altogether, accepting the authority of Man alone to govern his own affairs in the Universe. There were other ways into the Tradition, of course, which could be classed as magical or mystical, but these had always been very specialized approaches applicable to limited entrants only. As time went on, the latest approach along the Scientific line became of increasingly greater significance until eventually it dominated our Traditional theme almost entirely, and has not yet been supplanted.

III.

Science has come to stay as the major mark of our culture and civilization. Yet it is only a question of time before Science, having taken over the authority of religion, must also bear the blame for hampering human beliefs in the course of their endless questing for Light in Life. Science is wonderful, but it cannot give anyone a soul. Not all the science in this world will ever offer anyone immortal identity, and the spirit of life in us will not be satisfied with less. Sooner or later, science, like religion, will meet the condemnation of mankind because of its shortcomings. Then it will be the turn of an altogether new type of magic to help us spread our spiritual wings sufficiently to reach those realms of inner reality we have always sought for our true selves.

The highlights of the eighteenth century were concentrated on the phenomena then called "animal magnetism" and "somnambulism", now known as hypnosis and ESP or simply "psi." So-called "Black Magical" groups were working up a sizable Continental trade in sadistic sexual stimulation with a theatrical

Satanistic background. In England, wealthy youngsters called them Hell-fire Clubs and went in for group-sex for the sheer sake of erotic amusement. Commerce and culture had to compete with intellectualism, and religion was relegated to a back-seat position.

Starting with spiritualism, the nineteenth century produced probably the most extraordinary concentration of culture-expansion that has ever been known over ten successive decades during our whole history. All of a sudden, the issue of personal survival after physical death swept around the Western world. Boiled down to basics, ordinary living humans sought conscious contact with ordinary "dead" ones purely on a "person to person" arrangement of individual intelligence. Religion had really nothing to do with this latest development. It was an instinctive reaching out for reassurance that life could continue quite well without a material body to live in. Humans have always done this one way or another, but this time they were indifferent to what theologians or any other specialist said.

Despite all the conscious, unconscious, and other varieties of fraud and inaccuracies pervading spiritualism, it had a tremendous effect throughout the Western world. Due to improvements in communication, the practice spread through America and Europe with surprising speed. It was fundamentally simple. No expensive impedimenta were needed, just a few child's toys and the furnishings of any ordinary room. Furthermore it appealed mostly to the middle classes who had become by then the backbone of Western social structure.

Spiritualism was really a re-emergence of priestess-practice from the oldest times of a matriarchy, and its modern appeal was that it tended to restore at least a semi-religious authority among women. This was the era during which feminism was a rising force, especially in the United States. It was already throwing out challenges to male dominance in most fields of human activity, and so mainly from America in the last century came a stream of religious and occult influences putting women in prominent positions of importance within their frameworks. Later would follow Mrs. Eddy's Christian Science and Blavatsky's Theosophy, while back in Britian Mrs. Booth declared of her Salvation Army "My best men are women!"

Spiritualism started up a controversy which yet continues. Was it genuine or not? Fraud was certainly found, but there were instances, often recorded, which could scarcely be anything else than some kind of communication with unknown areas of inner intelligence. Opinions split in all directions and remain divided. The majority of initiated Western occultists were against spiritualism as interpreted by its popular practitioners. According to occult investigators, people were actually communicating with only the past personality parts of the deceased. After physical death, these artificial egos or "pseudo-selves" should normally be absorbed quietly back into the deeper and more spiritual levels of the identity. There it would be reduced to basic energy, ready for re-issue into incarnation again if the soul had not earned emancipation from earthly living. Interfering with this natural process hampered the progress of souls involved, and was of no real help to earth-based enquirers. Therefore, it was considered morally wrong to try dragging any departed soul back toward earth in the guise and character of its past personality. The thing to do was try and lift one's own spiritual level for even one instant high enough to make contact with the sought spirit beyond bodily boundaries altogether. Ethically correct as this may be, it aims rather above the heads of average people. So spiritualism as a movement stumbled along from one century to the next, though with lessening appeal proportionately to its organization as an established religion in its own right.

During the last century there were many attempts made at forming serious occult and magical groups or "Orders" functioning in full or semi-secrecy for the sake of spiritual security and non-interference from adverse or hostile influences. Most of these stemmed from Masonic procedures and principles, but were organized with some different formulae and symbology. For instance, the original modern "Druid Order" traces back to Stukely and some fellow antiquarians who were interested in concentrating upon what they felt were the rightful mysteries of their own country, rather than the mythology of Solomon's Temple and purely Herbraic folklore. The "Rosicrucian Society in England" stemmed from some scholarly men feeling a need to press ahead with philosophical research along lines of the eighteenth degree in Masonry. Already there were the beginnings of some Continental lodges run along Masonic lines which were accepting and initiating women, though these never received the slightest recognition from official British sources. Everywhere, ripples of excitement and anticipation of a glorious renaissance were running along the occult front.

It is mostly in literary ways that the inheritors of our Inner Tradition surpassed themselves during the last century. Brilliant and original books that have so far been unequalled for effect appeared in a steady stream. They are still classics of insight and scholarship, affording an inspiration and interest sadly lacking in so much modern mediocrity. Perhaps this may be because those really great books were never written for money or profit, but out of pure love for the subject and a creative consciousness within the writer bringing forth the work as naturally as mothering a child. We owe a great deal to writers of the nineteenth century who crystallized so much of our Tradition into words that will surely be with us for a long time yet. Nor should we forget those who spent lifetimes patiently collecting significant snippets from folklore preserved in the humblest homes. Nor others who saved fairy tales and legends from being lost to posterity. They have all earned their places in our Tradition for the remainder of its existence.

Quite a number of occult groupings were calling themselves "Hermetic Societies" of one kind or another. This title refers back to the "Trismegistic" sacred literature of early Christian times reputed to be a summation of all past secret wisdom mostly stemming from Egyptian and Greek sources. Hermes was the offical patron of such learning and therefore a suitable figure to represent those seeking to revive ancient mysteries in modern times. Then we have to remember the three general Paths to follow in pursuit of initiation. The Hermetic Path of intelligence on one hand, the Orphic Path of emotion on the other, and the Mystic Path of sheer spiritual aspiration for average intelligent Westerners to take. This covered all the studious branches of occult lore calling for an academic mind and a scientific approach as a rule. It also included elaborate and calculated ceremonial workings of a theatrical nature. Those are especially dear to the hearts of British people in particular, and Hermetic Lodges and Temples found natural homes in that country.

Probably the best known, due to publicity, was the Hermetic Order of the Golden Dawn, from the break-up of which so many lesser groups came into being. It was the original intention of the GD to become a corps d'elite consisting of highly cultured men and women from the fields of art, science, medicine, literature, and possibly politics, who would eventually be able to lead Western minds and souls away from the materialism and commercialism threatening to overwhelm our civilization. Its somewhat sad story should stand for a long time as a case-book example of how *not* to try and establish associations of occultists on earth, especially in the West. Yet the attention it attracted to itself rather than invited, aroused a great deal of interest in occult subjects among people whose concern had previously been casual.

By the end of the nineteenth century the Tradition of the West seemed to stand on the top of a pinnacle. Its culture was unchallenged, its expansion appeared assured and its continuity certain. Almost all the prophets were predicting a great and glorious Golden Age to come. Messiahs were imminent on every hand. Mysterious Masters were lurking around to lead hopeful humanity into wonderful realms of Love and Light. Spirits were spinning splendid stories about the New Age ahead, and expectations among esoterically minded people were virtually euphoric for the most part. Optimism and over-confidence abounded. But when Dawn finally did break, it was anything but Golden.

Nothing pushed pretentiousness harder off a higher horse than the first World War of the twentieth century. Unspeakably terrible as it was, that ghastly holocaust forced us into facing a lot of nasty facts about our own natures and exploded thousands of theories in all directions. In effect, the soul of Western man was suddenly stripped starkly bare of its insipid and futile impedi- menta and brought up sharply against the spiritual realities of its sick and sorry state. Yet it had to happen if there were to be hopes of our ever fulfilling the destiny in this world that our Tradition was directing us towards.

We invoked our Sacred Kingship to a degree never before supposed possible. Millions of young men sincerely believing their sacrificed lives would save the future of their families, friends, and nations, were slaughtered for the sake of political ambitions and the insatiable avarice of those controlling economic empires. The best of Europe's manhood were dying by thousands every day while the worst remained on earth to reap rewards of profit and power. Women wept everywhere and filled what wombs they could in order to offer their lost lovers and kinsmen a way back to the world again. It was a time of terror, trial, and tragedy for maids and mothers alike, yet on the whole they emerged from it with a new status and dignity that had been denied for many generations of mankind.

Out of this unspeakably horrible holocaust came forth a clear inner call for altered outlooks and approaches to the spiritual structures of our Tradition. Above all, we needed desperately to come far closer to its truth-track, nearer to its nature, from which we had been wandering away so stupidly. Though we did not altogether fail in this, our successes were then too small and insignificant to avert the avalanche building up again because the forces behind the War had not been fully played out, but had only paused for breath before the next break-out.

Whether that could have been diverted or avoided is anyone's guess. Certainly the "spiritual scene" on earth looked unpromising. There was a wave of popular spiritualism largely sponsored by those seeking consolation for their family losses during the war. If anything, the "spirit messages" were triter, more trivial, and sententious than ever. But it pleased many unhappy people with little else in their lives to cheer them. Various occult groups were starting up again, some of their leaders having returned from safe hiding places where they had doubtless prayed for the wicked world and the return of non-rationed times. A few were forthcoming who had seen war at first hand and were desperately hoping to start something on spiritual lines which might help avert or mitigate another such conflict. These, however, were much in the minority. Most meant to muddle ahead with what they had salvaged and make up a mixture-as-before medicine for all complaints of mind and soul alike.

There were exceptions. Notably Dion Fortune, otherwise Mrs. Pendry-Evans, made an outstanding attempt to introduce commonsense and a clear thinking attitude into Western occultism. Her approach was based on contemporary psychology and a program of procedure which tried to improve on Golden Dawn methods. The accent was very much on strongly disciplined behavior and developing a sense of individual responsibility toward Divinity and Humanity. She built up a background of very sound Western magical methods, drawn principly from Qabalistic, Christian, and Celtic sources. She left a legacy of interesting literature, some of her books still being classics. There is no doubt that her work had a most salutary influence on the Western Tradition, and those books will be memorials to her for a long time.

Between the wars, a peculiar period of confusion, uncertainty, and instability marked out our movements in psycho-social dimensions. We must remember the extreme pressures of poverty, alteration of standards, drastic changes of policies, increasing organization of a mass-media and radio-communications, and all other factors affecting our conditions of civilization. Who knew where anybody was going? Industrialism was overcoming our remaining rusticity, and the threat of the motor-car had been heard louder each week-end in the quiet retreats of our countryside. Aviation was already commencing its cacophony in the very air above our heads. To take a Tradition safely through all that turmoil was a problem few knew how to tackle because nobody had ever known it before. We know the rule of Life is "adapt or die", but that was the fastest rate of adaptation yet asked of mankind. Small wonder we went somewhat crazy in those times. Insecurity and insanity are often partners.

The echoes of World War One's explosions had hardly died away than those of World War Two began. Oddly enough, it began against a background of peace prophecies proclaimed from the "Spirit World." Scarcely a spirit or seer anywhere would admit war was only weeks away. Headlines of the psychic and occult publications were full of peace promises. Only an occasional astrologer uttered cautious forebodings. Even after the actual outbreak of hostilities, prophecies appeared that Hitler would drop dead, the war would be over in a short time. Afterwards they all invented ingenious excuses for their inaccuracies. "We did not wish to worry the world," or "We were not allowed to disclose disasters." Anything rather than admit ineffectuality, or something less than omniscience. Poor spirits! Their prestige was never the same again.

Once more the finest and fittest of young Sacred Kings fell, but this time there was a very noticeable difference of mass-attitude from that of the First War among British Westeners. Then, a sort of jingoistic hysteria was prevalent everywhere with waving flags, blaring bands, ecclesiastical exhortations to hate and kill every Hun in creation, and all the rest of the clap-trap. In the second instalment it was quite a different story. There was simply a grim determination to survive against the military might of another social system threatening established conditions in Britain and allied countries. Overall, the British were sad, sober, disillusioned, but utterly committed to what they felt was a life-and-death struggle for national survival. The Germans and Italians were wild with excitement and the certainty of conquest leading to enormous advantages of aftermath gains. However divided public opinion in America might be, the guiding policy was to make as much money from European belligerence as possible, then fix the best trading terms with the winning side afterwards. We must always remember that all antagonists involved were part and parcel of the Western Tradition up to that point, and therefore whatever they thought and did then has a long-lasting effect on us yet. Our deeply buried past is likely to influence our future more than might be suspected.

Germany had virtually won the war in Europe and fought the British to a stalemate, when Eastern intervention altered human history again. Firstly, Germany launched an attack against Russia, and secondly, the Japanese began hostility against America which forced that country into active alliance with the British as a consequence. This was now an East-West affair, and thus a clash between two opposite Traditions on inner levels. That is something likely to affect our future on earth to an extent which could be extremely serious for both. Especially in view of what happened, which eventually enforced an uneasy and somewhat unreal armistice upon antagonists.

This, of course, was The Atom Bomb, the most dangerous and destructive energy ever manipulated by man on earth. Physically, it means our world can be reduced to radio-active ruins in minutes, its millions of inhabitants incinerated in the hottest hell mankind has ever made for himself. Mentally and spiritually, its mere existence has altered us and therefore our Tradition forever on this poor planet. There is another and even more deadly danger the Bomb brought with it which seems to be unrealized except among occult individuals.

In some way not yet realized, all our radioactive explosions, experiments, and contrivances have made it possible for an altogether alien influence of what could be called "anti-life" to be drawn to us. This cannot be classed as "Evil" in any ordinary sense at all, and yet its long-term effects on us could prove fatal in the worst sense imaginable. It is inimical to our inner evolution purely out of necessity to itself rather than animosity to us, and indeed has no "feelings" of any kind whatever as we would recognize the word. What has happened is that our mishandling of fissionable elements opened up entirely unauthorized and automatic paths between our states of existence and what might be termed conditions of "contra-cosmos." These should never have had such direct connections with our evolutionary ecology. Extent of damage and possibilities of satisfactory repair-progams is undoubtedly engaging the attention of very esoteric experts, but what has already been done cannot be reversed. It must simply be coped with as best we can. The one certain point is that it threatens all our Traditions on earth equally, and therefore is something we will have to tackle together if we are ever to succeed as an evolutionary species.

So our last War ended on a very nasty note indeed. Nobody won it and everybody lost it. Worse still, it left us on a line leading to a future conflict between the Traditions of West and East, which could crash our civilizations and cultures completely. If this is to be actually avoided, an enormous amount of inner activity will be necessary. The important thing is that we should stay with the spirit of our own Tradition so that it presents no challenge to any other, yet consolidates the Way of the West within acceptable areas satisfactory for our survival, complementary to other cultures, and in a manner altogether necessary for the future of mankind per se. No other way will prove workable.

Out of the confusion following the last War came a tremendous upsurge of concern with magical and mystical matters, principly among the younger generation. Interest was mostly focussed on the need for expanded awareness, consciousness of other life-levels, empathy with other living orders, and achievement of identity as individual souls within a Cosmic Whole. Anything and everything of occult significance was dragged out of dust-covers and experimented with. In the twentieth century, medieval magical circles were traced again, old nature faiths were revived, often under the mistaken name of "witchcraft", pilgrimages were made along ancient tracks, to old stones and sites of primitive worship, and what was journalistically termed the "occult explosion" got into full swing with surprising speed. Magic was back again in a prominent position as a perfectly natural phenomena among young Western men and women. They talked it, read it, dreamed it, and to the best of their limited ability tried to practice it. Once more it was part of their lives. The whole issue was that now they had found these fascinating possibilities for themselves, what on earth were they supposed to do with and about them? That was the vital question nobody seemed very sure about.

5. Magic and the West

Western magic mostly consists of channeling consciousness through specific symbol systems connected to the spiritual depths of our Tradition. It is a two-way exchange. One end is operated objectively in our physical world by incarnate humans, the other by discarnate and non-incarnationary beings in different states of existence. These latter are concerned with the continuity and evolution of our common Tradition maybe more than we who are yet earth-embodied. Like us they are limited by laws controlling their life-states, and have to work within whatever force-frames apply to their range of activity. They are no more omnipotent than we are. Being closer to conditions of pure consciousness than ours, however, they are in a position to mediate and magnify our thinking through to deeper areas of awarenss. It is those forces which flow from inner levels that ultimately affect us on these earthly ones.

All this happens anyway, in the course of existence over a very broad spectrum of being. We should be concerned with the specific effects of working *intentionally* within the proper channels of consciousness linking us and our non-incarnate colleagues to our Western Inner Tradition. Behind that are remoter linkages leading to ultimates infinitely beyond our human status.

In earlier times it was simple. Initiate the enquirer into a West-working magical group and see what happened. Contrary to some current suppositions, such initiation confers no powers, privileges, or any particular abilities on anyone. To initiate means to start, nothing more. An initiated person is one who has been given a spiritual push, in order to start him going along some inner line of action. Traditionally, such an initiation amounted to bringing someone into close contact with the symbol-system concerned, suggesting a few simple exercises with them, then waiting to see what reactions followed from the candidate. Everything then depended on how he or she handled those symbols and elementary exercises. Were natural abilities and inclinations shown? Inventiveness and ingenuity forthcoming? Special talents displayed? Most importantly, was familiarity with the symbols evident, as if they awakened memories from previous incarnations or prior contact in other states of existence? Did they arouse genuine interest and a sense of attachment? Were their inner meanings picked up and grasped intuitionally or instinctively? It did not usually take very long for the circle to realize how their new companion was shaping up. Either he belonged with the West for certain and was worth training along those lines, or had no particular affinity with the Western Way and was best put upon some other path. Normally about a year's association would decide this issue quite definitely.

Nowadays this is not practical in general, although the principles still apply in particular instances. The older magical symbology of the West is no longer secret but available over a wide range of literature, art, and other cultural media. We are being carefully studied from spiritual levels to learn what we are making of ourselves with them. Studied by whom or what? Our own sort of souls who have advanced beyond embodied being, and interested intelligences of other orders who are sympathetic or otherwise to our evolvement as a species. To that extent, we are like specimens under test in a "Life-laboratory", except that we engineer the experiments in ourselves and automatically determine our destiny along such lines.

Therefore there is a very sound spiritual purpose behind the apparent shambles of our mis-named "occult explosion". Take a world full of bewildered, baffled, uncertain, and otherwise upset people in a state of dangerous instability. Shower down among them an entire cargo of symbols, notions, ideas, rumors, beliefs, and assorted spiritual stimuli. Observe carefully their reactions and behavior patterns with these, and they can soon be sorted into categories indicating the solution of their problems, which they must then find by their own initiative before they can ascend to higher Lifestates.

The "magical movements" of modern Westerners must be a fascinating sight to inner observers. How amusing the Cosmic joke of cultism running riot must be! The incredible inanities taken so seriously and sententiously with almost desperate determination, with every pathetic inadequacy of human nature disguised and distorted into something seeming important or influential. Poor little people playing magical make-believe for the sake of their pseudo-selves. Yet even the craziest or most curious behavior is of importance when studying the consciousness of any living species. There are also other areas in the same field that seem a lot more encouraging for our future prospects.

Here and there round the Western world are well-balanced and quietly competent operatives striving to pick up the scattered pieces of inner symbolism and build these into sound spiritual structures. This is usually an unspectacular and unostentatious business pursued privately. Not for the sheer sake of secrecy alone, but for several quite common-sense reasons. First, because such work has no appeal whatever for those seeking only personal aggrandisements and advantages, thrills and theatrics. Secondly because careful and painstaking work of this nature needs suitably secure and confidential conditions for its successful pursuit. Thirdly because there is nothing special to publish or publicize which could claim much attention from average readers. Bluntly, there would be no money worth having for promoters, publishers, and producers of literary, theatrical, and other forms of entertainment. For those reasons alone, modern magi of any integrity are unlikely to be disturbed greatly by glamor-grabbers.

What normal viewers would be interested to watch quite ordinary seeming men and women reading, writing, sitting still, walking the countryside, exchanging ideas, occupied with handicrafts, and visiting each other's homes? So much magic is accomplished under such commonplace circumstances. Even on ceremonially clothed and convened occasions, the attention of an outside audience would soon wander away from lack of sensual or suggestive stimuli. There are frequently fewer elements of entertainment in magical proceedings than afforded by a chess tournament. Action is all on the inside, taking place along lines that cannot be followed except by those accustomed to "working live" within those arcane areas.

What attracts most people to anything they might consider "magic" anyway? Basically, a search for self-fulfilment through what they hope will supply a short-cut to all they ask for. Deep down, they know they are deficient of so much needed to push them along the Path of Perfection. On more mundane levels they are conscious of social and other shortages demanding compensation. Maybe they are looking for money, friends, power, position, or whatever they think might provide them with a fulfilling self-state in this world. They also feel that, owing to circumstances and their own inadequacies, they are most unlikely to get very far by their own efforts and resources. They are asking for miracles. What they are really expressing is a fundamental urge from within to transform themselves.

That is indeed the finest function of magic within the Western Tradition, a means of self-transformation into something closer to the original Cosmic design behind each individual entity. Once that vital point is sufficiently grasped and assimilated, everything else will fit into perspective properly. All the odd practices, principles, and peculiarities of human behavior in connection with what people believe magic is will be seen as integrative items of an entire spiritual scheme bound up with our eternal struggle for survival and evolvement. Before we start looking for the "whats" of magic, it is essential to find the all-important *Why* within the soul of the seeker. Everyone should ask himself the blunt question: "What is so unsatisfactory with my own Self-state that I am asking a magical miracle to change it?" Or maybe the query could be phrased "Why is Divinity within me so dissatisfied with what I have made of myself so far?"

The fact that someone is attracted to magic at all automatically points to their inner awareness of inadequacy and a realization of need for compensative action assisted by higher than human orders of creative consciousness. There is nothing wrong with this whatever, providing it is recognized for what it is—a cry for help from Cosmos Itself. Where most people do go wrong, however, is in demanding all sorts of irresponsible and utterly impossible answers to their importunities. They are muddling magic with madness, and until they are able to distinguish one from the other they are unlikely to stay very sane or balanced on inner levels of life. Again and again they have to be taught how to stabilize themselves spiritually. Systems of Western magic are full of the needed formulae, but they take a great deal of devoted work and time to practice. Few people looking for magical marvels are prepared to sacrifice so much of themselves in such patient yet indispensible preparations for higher standards of spiritual life. So many are running rings around themselves expecting instant initiation into exclusive circles of self-importance. Later in life they wonder why they feel so exhausted and frustrated. Had they started seeking more sensibly in the first place, they could have told another tale altogether.

The obvious place to begin anything is with its first principles. In Western esotericism, this means its basic symbologies and their natural affinities with the Triple Pillars of Life. Through them, a prospective investigator must discover his own relationship with his "Real Self" or Inmost Identity. In order to do this effectively, he has to select the most suitable set of symbols to match his particular state of individuation. Not only must he feel certain that he positively *belongs* to and with the Western Inner Way, but he should feel sure of which special system within it he has to follow for at least the rest of his present incarnation. That is to say, he must have what was once called a "sense of vocation", a confident conviction that he is indeed choosing his proper pathway through life. Seldom an easy realization to reach on lower levels, once it comes through clearly, there is no denying its overriding authority over other considerations.

At one time, a systematic exposure to basic test symbols and some helpful working experience with them could have been effectively carried out in any competent Temple or Lodge. Now it is more a question of individual initiative in exploring those lines for oneself and determining by self-examination what reactions have happened. For instance, it is best to begin with the Western magical basics of the four Life Elements, Fire, Air, Water, and Earth, linked by the unique Element of Truth. Then bring in the equivalent symbols of Rod, Sword, Cup, Shield, and Cord. With the "Instruments", it is well to use actual physical emblems so as to gain an impression of solidity and actuality. What they really represent, of course, are the "Inner tools" with which consciousness itself is dealt and processed in our inimitable Western style.

Read about, make up, handle, and meditate upon these fundamental symbols. Devise small rituals, or use existing ones from other sources, and generally note inward impressions inclinations, and any relevant psychological findings. If there are signs of positive and progressive reactions, then further investigation is called for. If, conversely, the magical symbols stay dead in the hands of anyone, they are best relinquished altogether and different inlets sought elsewhere. About a year of experiment with these elemental symbols should be sufficient to make a definite decision possible.

As soon as enough empathy with the symbols has been experienced to make an affinity with Western magic certain, it is next wise to discover which, if any, special Western symbolic system offers maximum spiritual scope for the individual. This will depend largely on which of the three major Pathways applies particularly to the person in question. A broad selection of symbolic systems could be classified so:-

1.	HERMETIC (Intellectual)	Qabbalah and its ritualism, Rosicrucianism, Masonry, Illuminism, etc.
2.	MYSTIC (Aspirational)	The Grail workings, Abra-Melim, Trans-cendentalism, etc.
3.	ORPHIC (Emotional)	"Nature Magic", Dance and Drama devotions, Animism, etc.

In point of fact, modern Western magical practice tends to employ a blended mixture from all these speciality systems, but it is always best to realize one's own special link with the Tradition.

The simplest thing to do these days is read up on each topic and try to assess the inner appeal invoked thereby. Then take or work out an exercise based on each system, and undergo it as an actual experience, making notes or observation accordingly. A few months should cover the outlines of those systems in a very general way, and give good positive ideas of personal predelictions. For instance, a sensible work program could be patterened something like this.

1. Read up on Qabbalah, enough to gain some knowledge of the Tree of Life. Make a fair sized drawing of this with details. Contemplate diagram pinned to wall a few feet away by the light of three candles placed to line up with pillars of Tree. Recite aloud an invocation to the Archangels or similar piece, burning frankincense or some other incense. It is important not to attempt analysis of reactions at the actual time of doing this work. Wait until after a night's sleep, and then try a conscientious resume and assessment of effects.

2. Read literature on the Grail legend. Realize that no spiritual gains can ever be made without corresponding sacrifices on other levels. Face this issue inside the self and ask the "Grail Question": "Am I prepared to lose the whole world for the gain of a soul?" Do not come to a hasty decision, but let it dawn gradually as a conviction of one's own true inner character. Realize there is nothing to gain and everything to lose by making a false assessment. Attempting to "win the Grail" by any deliberate falsehood results in automatic loss of it indefinitely. This exercise can be made more realistic with the aid of a small "Grail chapel" in the shape of a chalice-like vessel containing a red glass lamp with floating wick just visible above the edge of the cup when sitting or kneeling before it. For better effect there should be a gauze veil hanging before the symbol so that it is seen in a somewhat hazy manner, preferably against a gold background. Devotional music may be used very quietly. The important thing with this exercise is that prayers and invocations should be impromptu and directed to the Divinity within oneself. Assessments should be made periodically, say once weekly.

3. Read up on magic related with nature. Make trips into countryside, "looking for God" in trees, stones, elements, and everywhere. Sing and dance invocations. Try to contact consciousness in other creatures. Go on expeditions to ancient sacred sites and meditate there, touching stones and trying to pick up inner impressions. Record reaction as inclination inspires.

Since the whole aim of these test experiments is to discover one's own natural niche in Western magic or otherwise, the most practical summary of them is probably an old-fashioned "quiz" demanding honest answers to very pertinent, probing questions. In the old days this would have been done under impressive Lodge conditions among robed companions before a solemn yet sympathetic panel of seniors. Replies had to be spontaneous, succinct, and clearly made. Nowadays an intelligent initiate is expected to show an ability for doing such groundwork out of his own imagination and inventiveness. It should not be beyond the scope of an average modern mind to construct an elementary quiz-pattern something on these lines:

1. Has this practice helped me at all? If so, how?
2. What was easiest about it?
3. What was most difficult?
4. Do I want to develop it further?
5. Has it made my life more purposeful? If so, how?
6. Would I like to share this with others?
7. Would I encourage others to try this? Why?
8. Do I look forward to the next occasion? How much?
9. How much would I miss the practice if unable to do it?
10. Did I feel aware in the slightest of any "invisible presence"? If so, on which occasions and where mostly?

Once it seems entirely certain which symbol system of the West is going to be followed, it must be positively adopted and put into regular practice. This means accepting its Master-symbol as a central concept and relating the associated concepts around it, forming a chain of consciousness capable of supporting the inner living of its initiates. Qabbalists claim with some justification to have done exactly this with the Tree of Life Master-symbol. The same principles could be applied to the Christian Cross, the Rose Cross, the Cosmic Cross, the Masonic Square and Compass, Druidic Triple Ray, Solar Stone Circle, the Grail Hallows, and so forth. If, as often happens, sympathies have been discovered for more than one system, then the Master-symbol of the most dominant should be adopted centrally, and links with the others fitted in where these naturally join up with connections to the Cosmic chain constructed.

What is of great importance is that when the central concept has been chosen and affirmed, only its natural and proper relative symbology will be used in connection with the conscious cosmos constructed around it. Indiscriminate mixing of the systems more or less haphazardly will do nothing except neutralize them all for whoever is foolish enough to make such a mistake. A system is a system and should be treated as such. Anyone supposing they will become a wonderful Western occultist or magician by attending a Qabbalist meeting on Sunday, a Rosicrucian one on Monday, a Druid gathering on Tuesday, and others on different days is simply wasting an incarnation on arcane amusements. First and foremost, it is necessary to be crystal clear just what and which system should be used to initiate one's own true Identity. When, and only when, this is satisfactorily set up and working inside oneself, it is allowable to develop confraternal linkages with other systems in ordinary ways.

The setting up of a central Symbol and arranging its associated correspondences around it is a major operation of Western magic. Although this has already been accomplished in our collective consciousness, every single initiate has to work out such a scheme for himself, thereby adding constant depth to the significance of our Tradition. Figuratively, the action is symbolized by the magician of popular belief tracing a chalk circle round himself and then invoking "spirits" from its center. Literally, it means constructing a cosmos of consciousness around one's own central nucleus of identity, then forming ideas out of that cyclic force which are expressive of spiritual relationships with life on all levels.

If we look again at our conventional magician in his circle we shall see that he has made a kind of psychic citadel. Outside the circle are all the hostile elements of existence, once called "demons", while in it the magus acts as directed by advisory "angels" who show him how to control and order those demons so that they will work for his benefit. The circle itself consists of "Divine Names", or symbols of directive control which have to be recognized and reacted with by magician, angels and demons alike. This fairy-tale presentation illustrated a profound truth of Western magic for those reading it in the right light.

To see the picture properly, we have to forget its external absurdities and find its internal accuracies. These show a human being intentionally surrounding himself with a protective perimeter of faith in order to make purely personal contacts and adjustments with environmental living. The hoped-for issue of this truly magical adventure is the advancement of individuality in the most favorable way possible.

Heaven knows we need protection enough just for staying alive in this world, against all that is inimical to human life and well being on every level. There is little use being physically and mentally protected while we remain vulnerable to adverse influences affecting our spiritual structures. The world inhabited by average humans can be an absolute hell of suffering for spiritually sensitive individuals unable to construct some form of protection for their inner identities. Most of us learn fairly fast how to build up a sort of "skin" around our secret selves which becomes a defensive barrier against external sources of injury. It is not so much that energies entering the self are injurious in themselves, as that individual reactions with them may cause damage to the soul concerned. We hurt ourselves inside ourselves far more than we are hurt by intentional ill-will from others. So we try and soften the blows of Life by insulating ourselves from its impact—if we can.

We do this by surrounding our innermost sense of identity and intention with a series of ideas on which we rely for preservation of self-position. In the case of a dedicated materialist, those ideas could be "My Money, my Social Status, my Mansion, my Cars, my Assets" and so forth. That sort of circle would be useless for anyone widely enough aware that its structure disappears immediately at physical death and has no reality past that fatal point. Any intelligent magician seeks a far more solid spiritual support. Nothing less than ideas relating to his own immortal and ultimate state of union with Infinite Identity will serve an initiated magician of the Western Way. If a consecrated circle can be constructed from those concepts, nothing that life or death can do will ever break it.

That is what the symbolism of "Divine Names" written around a conventional magical circle means. As chalk-inscribed letters they have no special powers whatever. As definite beliefs held in firm faith by whoever sets them up consciously as affirmations of existence, they have power to maintain the integrity of that individual against all adversities. The true significance of symbolic "Divine Names", therefore, is that they are sincere beliefs held by the magician regarding his own potentials as part of an infinitely greater Power. It does not mean that he believes his ordinary human personality is anything other than its limited being, or has any capabilities beyond that condition. It means that he is consciously aware of his inherent spiritual possibilities and self-significance, so he has surrounded himself with an appropriate symbology expressing such inner knowledge.

By itself, this protective perimeter is not enough. There is nothing to be gained by living as a human soul in splendid isolation from everything else in existence except one's own interior. Something has to be obtained from other sources which will make that interior worth living in. This means exchange of energies between oneself and those sources. The most sensible way of working this is through what amounts to filters or screens which only pass favorable frequencies between our external and internal conditions of consciousness, excluding injurious influences so far as practically possible. These need to be so designed that they will convert otherwise harmful energies into beneficial ones. Moreover, this effect should be two-way, so that not only incoming energies are altered for the better, but outgoing ones which might be injurious to others are also modified accordingly. There is no use protecting ourselves against outsiders if we are not prepared to protect them from our own hurtful emissions.

These specializing "screen-filter" constructions of consciousness are usually symbolized in Western circles by peripheral crosses. Those signify the meeting points of three great Circles theoretically traced around the magician horizontally, vertically, and laterally, to show the interlocking of Time, Space, and Event components of Cosmos. These nodal points of a magical self-system are often personified as Archangels, though they could, in fact, be represented by any other suitable concept fitting in with the general plan of whatever framework was set up. Since the "Archangel" arrangement has been dealt with in detail exhaustively elsewhere, there seems no need to labor it all over again here. What matters most is pointing out the principles involved. Here, we are considering the construction of a magical self-circle which inhibits ill-intentioned influences because of its inherent nature, yet is intersected by special contrivances permitting the two-way passage of helpful powers.

The Western system generally makes up these energy-adaptors in the form of humanoid Archangel-figures because it is easiest for humans to relate with something that resembles their own species. To begin with, they are built in the same way that a child invents invisible companions; i.e. by intelligent imagination and artistic skill. So first of all they will only process the consciousness of their creators in relation with whatever they represent as concepts. That in itself is useful enough, but with continued practice they will pick up and adapt external energies from other sources of consciousness so that these are reduced to suitable terms for their constructor to deal with favorably. Consequently life becomes much more meaningful and magical for that individual.

This scheme usually begins with a series of simple imaginative exercises calculated to develop control and application of consciousness in principle. For example, the trainee is told to place fingers and thumbs of both hands together at natural distance, then, gazing steadily between them, imagine he is holding a globe of pure shining light. This light is then imagined as becoming so intense the eyes have to be closed against it. Then it must be seen as weakening to a point of invisibility. All the colors from red to violet are visualized with varying degrees of light. After that, the same sphere materializes in the mind and changes from one substance to another in turn. All the different metals, for instance, followed by materials like wood, stone, glass, rubber, or balls of cotton, wool, silk, string, hemp, and so forth. These are mentally made to feel heavy or light as need be. Later with closed eyes, the imaginary sphere is held to the nose and various scents of all sorts called to mind. It is then held to the ear and sounds of different description evoked. It may be touched to the lips while tastes are thought of. The whole idea is to develop rapid and conscious assimilation of the sense-spectrum which supplies our means of constructing an appearance for whatever ideal is being invoked.

Exercises with consciousness like this are analogous to the scales and fingering of music. Once some skill is developed with "five finger exercises", more advanced practices may be attempted until it becomes possible to build up Archangel-figures with accuracy and rapidity. Eventually, these will grow into subjective reality to a point where simply thinking of their names will be enough to summon a sense of their presence. Gradually, they have to be artificially animated by categorized streams of consciousness from their creator. That is to say, a Michael-figure takes up all ideas of uprightness, resistance to evil, justice, magnaminity, and so forth. An Auriel-figure holds every notion of common-sense, caution, patience, tolerance, etc. A Gabriel-figure condenses compassion, feeling, love, forgiveness, sympathy, and so on. A Raphael-figure deals with alertness, keenness, intelligence, and the like. A Metraton-figure should cope with all ideas relating the individual with higher orders of life up to Divinity, and the complementary Sandalaphon-figure deal with all lower orders down to Divinity again. Connecting all these figures is the mysterious and unfixable Suvuviel, representing no less than Truth itself which links all levels of Life everywhere, yet we can never determine its exact nature anywhere.

At first, of course, such constructions of consciousness exist purely in the minds of their makers. Yet because they are recognized archetypes within the Western Tradition, they exist in quite a large number of like-working minds, and so share a telepathic link in common. More importantly still, they connect with corresponding types of inner intelligence deriving from higher than human sources, and therefore put their constructor in closer touch with superior sorts of spiritual beings willing to help humans climb the ladder of Life and earn emancipation into Light through evolution. These do not in any way run mortals' lives for them or take over responsibility for human affairs in our world to the slightest degree. Their function is to offer spiritual opportunities for us to take advantage of if we will. They do that much in any case, but the Archangel constructions allow us to co-operate consciously rather than instinctively in this scheme.

Built up in this way through a partnership between incarnate initiates and other orders of being in different dimensions, such Archangel-figures or whatever concepts may be constructed are technically known as Telesmic Images. The more accurately they represent the inner realities they symbolize the better. Perhaps it would be natural to wonder why a single great inclusive Figure of a Christ-concept or Deity-Aspect would not serve better. That could indeed be used as a focal approach to Inner Life, but the importance of the Archangelic idea lies in its *patterning* around the individual as nodal points of categorized consciousness. That is the key to the whole Western way of working. It is the pattern itself which produces results, just as definite arrangements of figures or codes connect us with other humans on earth. There are telepathic lines of communication as well as telephonic ones, and if we ring the right number alone either, we can expect an answer, albeit in different ways.

An attempt at Christianizing the scheme was made a long time back and is sometimes called St. Patrick's Breastplate. It is an invocation that runs:

> Christ be with me, Christ within me,
> Christ behind me, Christ before me,
> Christ beside me, Christ to win me,
> Christ to comfort and restore me,
> Christ beneath me, Christ above me,
> Christ in quiet, Christ in danger,
> Christ in hearts of all that love me,
> Christ in mouth of friends and stranger.

This is a very lovely and consoling verse, but doesn't have the precision and exactitude of the cosmic construction produced by careful work with the Archangel arrangement. At the same time, there is nothing to stop any dedicated Christian from using the Circle-cosmic pattern by forming it with specific attributes of the Christ concept to suit the quarters in question. For instance, instead of Archangels, a Christian could build up a magical cosmos around himself somewhat in this fashion:-

> Be the Divinity of Christ above me,
> Be the Humanity of Christ below me,
> Be the Guidance of Christ before me,
> Be the Support of Christ on my right,
> Be the Compassion of Christ behind me,
> Be the Protection of Christ on my left,
> Be the Truth of Christ around me,
> Be the Spirit of Christ within me.   AMEN.

That would equate the fundamentals of the entire scheme into Christian symbology. Since the actual pattern is much more important than the description of Divinity attributed to its points, a Christian magical Cosmic circle would be quite workable if made up this way.

There is nothing really to stop anyone from making up these magical images as any sort of "spirit-guide" they fancy, and taking a chance on what, if anything, animates it from Inner dimensions. It seems that very many so-called "guides" are made through this process. The trouble is that unless some kind of fool-proof filter is built into them, they may easily be manipulated by unreliable or malicious classes of consciousness. That is why it is best to remain with proved and reliable patterns like the Archangels, which have become a fairly standard Western procedure.

What happens when such a magical circle is duly set up and got into going order by means of meditative and ritual practices? If this job is properly done, the circle should start producing its own results by reactions through its initiator. All required "Inner teaching" or contacts with higher consciousness ought to come through the specializes circuitry of the magic Circle, so that each soul in its own circle receives exactly what it should in the way of spiritual guidance, encouragement, or other inner influences according to its needs.

This is why the ground plans of most reputable occult Temples in the West have a similar formal layout of a circle-cross design with central altar and appropriate represenations at the Quarters. The main function of any Temple is to show symbolically how we have to arrange the spiritual side of our beings in actuality. Most magical Temples of the West are usually patterned on a Cosmic Cross system because that happens to be our special way of individuation. Within that overall scheme, the various symbols connected with the rite being worked are related meaningfully with each other according to the nature of the ceremony in question. Yet, unless participants actually do the same equivalent things in their own spiritual structures, nothing magical happens at all. The real magic does not lie in the symbols, but in one's personal relationship with what those symbols represent.

Once again, we are brought back to the basic tenet of our Western Tradition, the Sacred King sacrifice, this time in a modern magical manner. Nowadays it is an action taking place within a single self. The "King-part" of an individual soul sacrificed by the "Priest-part" of that same being for the sake of the "True Self" they intend to become. This could indeed be described as the "Mass of the Holy Grail" in practice and principle. It aligns with the central Pillar supporting the entire structure of

Western magic. Orphic and nature rites belong to the right hand Pillar, and Hermetic intellectual activities to the Left. Properly understood and practiced in a magical manner, this modern mystical version of the Sacred King concept is the genuine inner interpretation of the so-called "Self-sacrifice" needed to save us all within the Tradition of the West.

The implications of this are so stupendous that few may grasp much of their significance. There is yet to come an entire "New Wave" in the Western magical movment. It will be rooted in these ideas and provide techniques enabling people to work out their own salvation according to their individual needs. Not that there will be very much "new" involved, except fresh formulas for coping with ageless concepts. Looking back through our past, we can see that each era produced its own adaptations of magic which, by subtle alterations within consciousness, helped alter the course of our history. This is true today, and perhaps a cynic might be forgiven for wondering whether all the magic in the world can change the dooms we seem determined to invite on ourselves. No magic averted our wars, though perhaps those horrific happenings altered our magic for the better. Can our contemporary magic preserve us from the perils of our pseudo-peace? It can at least be geared to play its proper part in our perfection program, and that is what present practitioners should be chiefly concerned with.

It is probable that the actual percentage of whole-hearted workers with Western magic in each generation is very small indeed, possibly less than one percent of the population. All that makes them unique is what they do with their consciousness, and how this affects others. Perhaps it sounds like an enormous expenditure of effort poured into a project that promises little in the way of appreciable returns. Only those who really value the spiritual significance of what they are doing are likely to persevere past the point of dividing disappointment from discovery. The failures will fall away from sheer lack of perceptible returns and unrewarded ambitions. None but patient and persistent practitioners go steadily along through the same and worse obstacles toward inner truths only seen from very exalted states of awareness.

There is no use looking back for encouragement by wonderful "success-stories" among past practitioners of magic in our

Tradition. All we shall see there are apparent martyrs and misunderstood men and women living somehow out of context with their times. Who, *by magic alone,* made huge fortunes, reached pinnacles of power, or otherwise achieved what this world calls "success"? We shall find the majority of them had very troubled lives and often sad ends. Sometimes they managed some kind of brief and ephemeral triumph usually in early middle life, then declined from that point to whatever death released them from bodily bondage. In many cases, it was only a long time after their deaths that their significance was realized by others to any marked degree. Mostly, their very names were unknown except to inner intelligences. Yet one way or another, they have left indelible impressions on our spiritual genetic depths which will influence their magical descendants for a very prolonged period ahead.

6. Towards the Temple

Assuming one is both interested and devoted enough to pursue a personal and practical path of magic within the Western Tradition, how would that person proceed? That is indeed a prize problem. Only tentative answers in general terms can really be attempted.

First and foremost, of course, comes the all important question of "vocation". Are, or are not, the souls concerned really prepared to sacrifice the mainstream of their lives to service in the cause of our common Tradition according to the magical "Line of Light within the West"? Do they fully understand and accept the responsibility and consequences of what they intend doing? Are they really aware of what they are taking on themselves? And are they willing to endure and experience whatever may be demanded of them on all levels of Life as a result of their decision? This is truly a terrible "Grail Question" which sooner or later has to be faced by all who would enter the real "Mysteries of the West" on deeper than surface levels.

What this amounts to is, are we born with magic "in our blood" or do we merely want to make its acquaintance on purely social terms as a matter of inquisitive interest? Authentic Western magi mostly "have it in their blood' as an inheritance from former lives, very often persisting through familial lines. These are relatively rare and seldom conspicuous to any extent. They neither proclaim themselves publicly, nor welcome recognition outside very limited circles. Nor do they depend on commercial courses of instruction, membership of "Occult Orders", or other forms of assistance for developing their intrinsic abilities. Whatever they need will automatically grow out of the necessity itself because of their inner connections.

On the other hand, there are undoubtedly many souls who may not be so advanced in the Tradition, yet would most sincerely want to be of some service to it within limited ways according to their circumstances and abilities. Such service is often of very great value; sometimes of inestimable value. It may be that an individual might only produce a single instance of service in a whole incarnation, yet no one else could have done just that, and without it the entire Tradition would have been so much the poorer. Nothing that fills a specific need can be considered unimportant.

At one time, the whole field of occult activity was visualized as a sort of nuclear arrangement consisting of concentric circles wherein all classes of souls sorted themselves into their natural orders. Beyond the outer limits was "The Wilderness" where souls just strayed around more or less aimlessly until they started looking toward something they vaguely felt was a Spirit or "God" calling them into Itself from a long way off. After many mistakes and false starts, they eventually found their way into an "Outer Court", wherein souls like themselves were seeking the same thing with a certain amount of skill and determination. Nevertheless, they were still extremely fallible and imperfect. It often took a long time to work this lot towards the center to enter the next circle of Inner Initiates. These had much clearer ideas of what they were doing and how to keep the whole thing going for everyone's benefit. They realized their limits only too well, and were prepared to work unreservedly for the Cosmic Cause they felt so closely. Within the next circle were still more evolved souls, and so on until the Absolute Center was reached, and then THAT was THAT! Today, our "Outer Courts" are figurative, and indicate a conglomeration of people with aims in common, sorting themselves out before making more direct and determined tracks towards whatever truth they have perceived by their own inmost light.

Sooner or later, those who sat down quietly to think things out while others ran rings round them, were bound to reach some observant conclusions. They began to see that we live in "fields" of common consciousness which we have to share with each other in much the same way as we all have to breathe the same ocean of air, or utilize the same electro-magnetic energy of this earth. Consciousness as an energy exists around us, within us, and ultimately constructs us. People are its "phenomena", so to speak. Yet, although it is ubiquitous per se, it has categorical classifications in the way radio frequencies can be considered as "bands". As humans, we can cover only a limited range of these. In that range, the broadest sections are receivable by all humans, but as the frequencies become higher and finer, only the most developed and evolved types of our species can deal with them. At the "top end" of our spectrum, consciousness goes right beyond our present reach altogether. We can only keep contact with other beings using such energies by means of mutually acceptable symbolism. Neither our brains nor minds originate consciousness of any kind. They simply interpret it for us on bodily and intellectual levels respectively.

The vast majority of humans receive and react to consciousness in various ways according to their characteristics. We are influenced spiritually, mentally, and physically by the common atmosphere of awareness we share. Whether we like the idea or not, we are all undoubtedly existing in an ambience of consciousness which has been used, misused, processed, polluted, and otherwise altered or interfered with by every human capable of changing its currents in the slightest way. This is a very serious matter once its full implications are realized. Our very lives literally hang on its present and future effects on us.

As a rule, few humans have much ability to take up consciousness intentionally, process it in themselves, and alter it specifically so as to push it on its way again with some positive purpose. That in itself is an act of pure magic, whether seen as such or not. In our very early days, only a minute majority of mankind could do anything at all like this. Those naturally became leaders of families and tribes, priests, kings, prophets, and so forth. The consciousness they processed provided a pool serving their people for centuries, until successive generations began to develop the art for themselves in ever widening circles. More and more humans individuated to degrees where they became capable of changing consciousness on their own initiative, thus influencing others. Those who realized what they could do and how it had to be done became practitioners of magic, in *fact* if not in title. Now, after long lines of cumulative effects, we have come to a crux where the mass-mind of mankind is being pressurized beyond belief by experts who would gladly enslave it for their own purposes of power and profit. Alternately we are entitled to an option of enfranchizement into individual states of spiritual self-government which our incarnations on this earth have fairly earned for us. This is where the truly vocational Western mage enters the inner arena.

His or her self-structure has been so arranged that all ambient consciousness can be accepted, treated, and then re-circulated in far more suitable condition to serve the spirit of the Tradition. Additionally, initiates of this status automatically radiate the frequencies of consciousness needed by less advanced humans in order to aid their evolutionary efforts up the Ladder of Life.

It is chiefly souls of such stature who keep the fundamentals of our Inner Tradition continuing more or less on course. They are like the vital "trace elements" of our bodies which are almost undetectable, yet without them we would surely sicken and die. Not all are purely magicians by any means. Artists, musicians, poets, writers, and all classes of consciousness-processors are involved. Yet none of them could operate effectively without the support of non-incarnates on one hand, and a "fellowship of faith" among humans on the other. Once more, as always, we are back to the Priest-King principle of mediation between Humanity and Divinity. That is the unique position of those faithfully dedicating their lives to magical and other branches of belief connected with our Western Inner Way. It is certainly true that such offered lives have to be laid down in very different methods to those of olden days. No miraculous births, privileged lives, and spectacular deaths await modern mediators; only ordinary incarnations spent in faithful and devoted service to a Tradition for the sake of the Spirit it stands for. These incarnations are often very difficult and dangerous, or maybe just dull and apparently quite unrewarding. The decisive factor is that these dedicated souls are needed to be in specific situations to provide some definite and indispensible service. So what is any sincere soul to do if it really intends uniting with the magical part of our Tradition in modern times?

Many enquirers, especially young ones, get wonderful ideas about finding incredible "Mystic Brotherhoods." Marvellous and mysterious operations of super-powerful "Orders" are imagined, led by "great Occult Masters", having all the secrets of life and death in their keeping. They suppose initiation into these must lead to almost instant personal promotion and spiritual importance. Most humans have ideas of this kind they express in different ways. In old times people hoped their Sacred Kings would save them from a lot of sad experience. Christians believe that their Divine Victim saves the souls of all mankind forever, if the offer is accepted and followed up. Many people now believe that their political and social systems are saving them from all sorts of responsibilities and difficulties. Throughout the ages, it has always been the same story in changed clothing.

It might be well for would-be magi of the West to learn as soon as possible that fairy-tale "Magical Orders" or like secret associations for promoting personal powers simply do not exist as such, apart from wishful thinking. There are plenty of secret organizations in existence for various reasons. The "Mafia" is an obvious example. There are also quite a number of groups all claiming different degrees of occult importance in the West, some sincere, others only time-wasters, others again nothing but money-grabbers. Sooner or later, people seriously interested in Western occultims come up against the perennial problem of whether or not to join in with some group, cult, or association, and all must make their own decisions for themselves on this point. A few guiding lines might be helpful.

In the first place, examine personal motives for wanting to join any group very carefully indeed. If these are derived from average needs for meeting other humans of similar interests, finding suitable sex-partners, spending amusing evenings, making advantageous contacts, or "one-up-manship" of any sort, then all this and far more may be better found in various social clubs. If the motive derives from a wish to witness wonder-working and spectacular spiritual activities, that is doomed to disappointment and disillusionment from the start. As a rule, approaching any human association with absurd or impossible expectations is simply asking for trouble of all sorts. So many people do exactly this, and learn the hard and humiliating way, usually without more serious results than loss of money, time, and illusions. Sincere and honest self-appraisement would have saved them all their trouble.

The best way to look at occult societies and groups is through the view-finder of common sense. For instance, if some concern is advertising widely for members, they have something to sell and are seeking no more than customers. Now what is the absolute most that they, or any other so-called occult organization could possibly supply for money? Distributed information certainly. In these days, no more than could be obtained from public libraries. For those without abilities or facilities for research, that service might be worth paying exorbitant fees to obtain—or it might not. Another sales item can be classified as entertainment and accessories. Elaborate ritual productions and equipment, robes, regalia, decorations, initiation certificates, and all the rest of the romantic paraphernalia so beloved by thrill-seekers. Harmless, but highly over-priced collectors' commodities. Apart from such offers, there may be fringe benefits like conducted tours of sacred sites, conventions with lectures and banquets, plus the usual trimmings expected of modern organizations during their social gatherings. All these amenities cost money which many are well prepared and most willing to pay, but they cannot possibly be any more than expensive entertainments however they are disguised. All that can be done is to show people how to connect themselves together in order to make the most of what they can reach for themselves. The rest is a matter of encouragement and simple fellowship. Any association or group offering no more than this might at least deserve attention from enquirers.

In fact, it is best to distrust any organization which refuses to state plainly in the simplest terms exactly what its constitution is, its aims, requirements of members, and regulation of affairs. It should scarcely need to be said that no papers or documents ought to be signed by applicants without the closest scrutiny and care. If in the least doubt it might pay to consult a lawyer, because signed promises concerning membership fees or other expenses have legal force. Then, too, members may be liable for heavy costs if claims are made against their society, unless they are protected by specific clauses. No commitments whatever should be made that cannot be terminated by a formal letter of resignation. Fantastic or illogical "initiation oaths" demanding unquestioning obedience under pain of idiotic penalties should never be agreed to, no matter how much "matters of form" are pleaded. Anything contrary to codes of conscience and civilized behavior ought to be firmly and unhesitatingly rejected by anyone unwilling to behave in such ways of their own accord.

There is, perhaps, a rather prosaic point worth mentioning here in connection with "Occult Groups". They are normally "checked out" by the police who are purely looking for actual illegalities or contraventions of civil codes. Most of them may be harmless enough from a police point of view, but they can still be undesirables from inner angles. Here and there they may be involved in criminal concerns which have escaped police notice for various reasons. The average enquirer is highly unlikely to encounter these, or be approached to join them. As a rule, the more evil a group is, the more exclusive it becomes.

Another point is that most Governmental services, civil or otherwise, take a generally poor view of their members who show any marked interest in the occult. In official eyes, this indicates "unreliability", or some uncertainty of unquestioning devotion to imposed duties. The last thing Chiefs of Staff want in their ranks are people interested in individuation outside officially allowed areas. This means that anyone known to have occult inclinations will be carefully marked as such on private dossiers which they never hear of. Though no obvious official notice is taken, there can be quite a lot of disadvantageous repercussion. For example, promotion may be delayed, or postings made to unwanted places, or any other of the many methods employed by services everywhere to deal with their less approved members. Therefore, if even minor members of Government services are seriously considering occult interests and activities, they would be well advised to keep this as closely confidential as possible.

An important thing to bear in mind is this. The only genuine justification for the existence of any Western esoteric organization in this world is for assisting its initiates to "stand on their own spiritual feet". This means to show them how to individuate so that they will have no need for earth-based Temples or Lodges any more. That is one reason why a first-joined Lodge is affectionately called a "Mother", because a mother raises her sons to grow up and live independent lives elsewhere. In a sense, Western training Temples should be considered as nurseries and preparatory schools, with the purpose of guiding humans along lines of life leading to adult responsibility in wider and much more demanding areas.

Therefore, even the finest occult Lodges and Temples imaginable on mundane levels could only help entrants just so far upon their Inner ways. Sooner or later comes the "parting point" where initiates have to seek their solitary "truth-tracks" through Inner Space in search of whatever target they have set themselves. There is a lot of parallelism between launching a space-ship and sending a soul off towards its "Self-star". At the present time, a huge organization is needed for getting a single ship away from the ground, but eventually ships will be able to come and go entirely with their own facilities. So, while in times gone by it took a large combined operation to start or "initiate" souls on evolutionary expeditions, most of them are now capable of commencing on their own accounts.

Over the centuries, most of the intimate circles of Western initiates have learned by hard and sad experience to exclude anyone at all who does not harmonize properly with their particular power-patterns. They simply cannot afford to have their painstaking work ruined by incompatibles. However much they might be willing to admit other suitable souls it will be a long time before they are likely to make tentative signs of welcome. First, there would have to be unmistakable evidence of sincerity and suitability, then a sort of screening process for determining capability. In the end, there has to be an unanimous decision whether or not to offer the candidate an opportunity for probationary admission. Traditionally in the West no one is supposed to be openly asked to join an initiatory circle of companions. Application must be made entirely of their own accord and free-will. What usually happens is that discreet hints are given that such an application would be considered sympathetically. Even a hint of that kind is only to be given once, and no pressure whatever must influence the candidate's voluntary decision.

At one time, among esoteric circles, there was a custom that candidates were allowed three applications. If rejected on the first ballot, they were informed of this, and told they could apply again if they were willing to accept far more stringent terms of entry. Should they agree, and the second application failed, they were given a last option of entry under really strict or unpalatable conditions. If they still insisted despite the awful warnings, then they had to be provisionally admitted under the terms laid down and there was nobody to blame but themselves if things went wrong. From that point it became a case of character training, commando style. It is doubtful if there were many admissions of this type, though it is said A.E. Waite was admitted to the Golden Dawn on such conditions. Nevertheless, it is still customary and advisable to try discouraging and putting off all eager enquirers. If they are patient and persistent, continuing approaches quietly and confidently, they will find acceptance in the end, while if they are easily brushed off and dissuaded, they would be unsuitable souls for serious spiritual work, anyway.

In modern times, however, there is neither much need or obligation to join up physically with any organization on earthly levels in order to follow the magical workways of the Western Inner Tradition. In fact, those with truly deep motivations would be best advised to avoid physical contact with "organized occultism", and concentrate on making their own links directly with Inner associations. Each individual must learn how to live as if they themselves were a fully fashioned and operative Temple having a complete quota of members, and following the rules and procedures of customary magical practice. In other words, a spiritual system and discipline has to be set up and kept going according to whatever Inner order the soul in question intends to arrange within himself.

Many people might suppose it indispensible to construct an actual magical Temple perhaps in some spare room of a house and conduct elaborate ceremonies therein. However pleasant and enjoyable that might be, it is not essential at all. The main function of Western Magical Temples is to show symbolically how practitioners are supposed to arrange themselves inside themselves. Real Magical Temples are factually the spiritual state of our own inner beings. Once the general ground-plan and lay-out of a Magical Temple is known and understood, anyone with knowledge could reproduce such conditions in themselves at will, providing adequate efforts at constructive imagination and concentrated consciousness had been made. That is true enough, even though relatively few people are prepared to spend the time and energy on such work. At first it is arduous and unrewarding, but gradually it improves and can even be fascinating. So many aspirants give up during the dull stages, however, being unwilling to sit still physically while becoming intensely active inside themselves, working on the practical job of constructing a conscious Temple.

The typical pattern of Western Magical Temples is very simple and should be widely known, but a brief capitulation here may be helpful. A Magical Temple of the West is really a set of alignments providing a practical plan for constructing one's own Self-cosmos. These alignments are symbolized through the three components of Cosmos as we percieve them—Time, Space, and Events. Space is symbolized by a ceiling design representing Heaven, and a floor design depicting Earth. This upright alignment signifies the relation of an individual initiate with Divinity and Humanity, plus all the lesser orders of Life. Time is shown by the four walls having a decor suggesting the seasons; Spring in the East, Summer in the South, Autumn in the West, and Winter in the North. Each wall bears its appropriate Magical instrument in some suitable setting. Events are symbolized by the rites themselves, taking place in relationship to the central altar.

This altar is normally of double cube proportions, usually a wooden cupboard in which some of the sacred vessels or symbols are kept. It is covered with a large square cloth having corner tassels hanging almost to the ground. Sometimes the cloth simply drapes across two sides about halfway down, and a frontal to suit seasons or occasions faces the working position. An altar is always considered "horned" at its corners. Occasionally there may be actual animal horns attached, customarily rams' or bullocks' horns. These are reminders of the incalculable debt we owe the animal kingdom for all the sacrifices we made of them in order to build up our civilization. Untold millions of them have died so that mankind lived. Not only horned beasts, of course, but every kind of creature. Then we have to remember that animal sacrifice was substituted for human life long ago, until our present vegetable sacrifice (bread and wine) supervened. So horns are sometimes still seen on modern altars as memorials, or else symbolized as tassels or other decorations. Around the horns is often looped a cord, symbolizing the universal tie of Truth binding life together. It is also a reminder that sacrificial victims were once tied literally upon altars, as we must now bind ourselves metaphorically by obligations and duties to the basis of our own beliefs. In some cases a decorative floral border runs round the altar top, in memory of the garlands customarily placed on the heads of Sacred Kings and later their animal surrogates, shortly before their sacrifice. Originally, every flower and leaf had its own paritcular meaning, and the whole garland itself was a prayer and benediction. Today, a faint memory of this continues in vases of flowers placed on altar tops, mostly in churches. A magical altar more often bears a lighted lamp to signify the Spirit whose Divine sparks we are, although this lamp may be of the hanging variety above the center of the altar. This leaves the altar top free as a working surface for the symbols being employed as foci for the force-flows in progress during the rites.

In Western practice, the altar and its symbolism stands for the central principle of self-sacrifice, correctly understood, which is the focal point of our whole spiritual structure. It signifies the Priest-King, or "Melchizadekian" function of our magical Initiates. The "animal" sacrificed on such an inner altar is the lower side of our own natures, and moreover it has to be a willing victim, offering itself out of pure love alone. Such is the central concept around which Western Magical Temples are built. Considered in one sense, it is the Holy Grail idea in practice. However interpreted, it is certainly the essential meaning in our lives which holds all else together as a cosmos in common. A Temple without an altar would be no more than a museum. The altar is the pivot upon which everything turns as a dynamic relationship between Divinity and Humanity.

There are many other items of ritual equipment used in Western Temples but they only provide supporting symbolism. Perhaps an exception is the Pillars, a pair of cylindrical uprights, one black and the other white, usually some seven to eight feet high. They symbolize the alternate extremities of Life, between which initated individuals must become as mediating middle Pillars of Perfection. They are constant reminders that we should always live and work so as to balance and harmonize ourselves between oppositional forces. Another major item is the Standard, representing whatever Master-Symbol the Temple serves. This could take any form from a banner to an elaborate sort of shrine. Its task is to show whichever aegis of the West is being worked under. Thus a Temple devoted mainly to Qabalah would show a Tree of Life standard, a Rosicrucian one the Rose-Cross, and so forth. In some more modern Western Temples, there is a growing tendency to place the altar into a Western position, with the Standard behind and above it, and the Pillars before it, thus making a sort of sanctuary concentrated into the West. The center of the Temple is then marked by a straight Staff signifying "Heaven-Earth" pivotal linkage.

There may not be many modern Westerners able to furnish and operate a physically working Temple entirely from their own resources. A large number probably cannot find a quiet corner in their accommodation for a few minutes meditation. That is why Western practitioners have had to learn the art of self-insulation, so that they are able to take their own Temples around with them constantly. It is not easy, but with enough practice it becomes natural and indeed essential for maintaining some spiritual sanity amid so-called civilized living on earth. Almost anyone can have spiritual feelings when situated in the special atmosphere of a Temple or church. It takes real magical skill to create such conditions in themselves amid the racket of modern airports, railways, or motorways. One is reminded of the old-time orators training, putting pebbles in the mouth while standing on a seashore close to roaring waves. They then had to learn how to speak so as to be heard clearly above the din. That is similar to what would-be magi are faced with in our sort of world. Nothing but patient and persistent work over maybe many years will develop this art to any dependable degree.

The only possible way to construct this vital "Temple not made with hands" is by determinedly spending sufficient time and effort each day at building it bit by bit with creative imagination. This should be at regular periods, such as ten minutes morning and evening. It is best to make out a methodical "building program" with the help of a notebook, so that the whole structure is covered systematicly. For instance, one wall might be imagined on each occasion so that all four were covered in two days. The door is at the North East angle, which is the point of exit and entry at the end of Winter and the beginning of Spring. Then a ceiling representing the heavens, and a floor depicting earth can be added next time. The ceiling is often blue with a central Solar symbol, and floors may have anything from intricate maze-patterns to conventional checkerboard squares, even ordinary floral designs. Day by day, something else can be added. The major Instruments; Sword, Rod, Cup, Shield, the Cord. Then the altar, item by item. Then the Pillars, and the Standard. Everything has to become clear enough in consciousness to be seen, felt, and experienced in use as if it were solid and physical. That is the really important part of the exercises.

It should scarcely need to be said that this work is nothing whatever like "day-dreaming". That is merely a matter of allowing the mind to graze, as it were, on pastures of its pleasing fancies. Magical exercises consist of controlling consciousness with will for positive purposes. In the case of this Temple-making, it is an essential part of the Western Tradition, because it creates energy patterns along Inner lines which attract the attention of other Life-orders associated with us in spirit. The same work would have to be done by individuals if they had physical access to magical Temples every day of their lives. Nothing can ever substitute for the Temple we all have to make within, and, actually, of ourselves.

Perhaps the most vital point to realize during these workings is that the symbols employed represent real qualities of being which we are supposed to develop and use in our own selves. For instance, there is nothing magical in waving a sword around. There is great deal of magic in calling up and employing our inherent "Sword qualities" of keenness, flexibility, precision, etc., to suit spiritual situations. The physical symbol is valid only insofar as it helps us invoke and use its inner counterpart in our own characters. So with each Temple symbol, a corresponding spiritual quality has to be identified and focussed in the consciousness of the constructor. Visualising and mind-forming the finest Cup imaginable is insufficient by itself. With this action must go feelings of love and compassion, a capacity for being filled by inspiration, and every inner ability associated with the Cup-symbol. That is what making a Temple of ourselves means.

Even the finest Temple ever made, however, would be inadequate by itself. We are all surely aware of "atmospheres" held by Temples, churches, and other condensers of spiritually directed consciousness. One has only to enter such localities to sense their "charge". They vary from an intense to an inert degree of inner influence. This is entirely due to the workings of consciousness within the area over a persistent period of systematic practice. Moreover, it is the result of exchanges between human and other classes of consciousness. The purpose of a Temple, after all, is to provide facilities for communication between Huamanity and Divinity, contact with one's own Higher Self. The Temple also provides concious links between ourselves and other types of Life that are willing to help us advance along our particular path of spiritual evolution.

Contacts of such a nature become possible only because of constant focusing of consciousness in regular and rhythmic fashion. We have to set up a series of energy-impulses which may then be modulated by the contacting consciousness. The actual mechanism of this can be studied in the use of "mantras", or repetitive formulas such as those employed in the case of a rosary. On low levels of awareness, the participant directs attention into producing an intense and rhythmic chain of impulses formed from pointed prayers. Given sufficient potency and persistence, this action automatically produces a "peak-pattern" recognizable by inner intelligences able to receive human—generated frequencies of consciousness. If willing to respond, the normal procedure is to beam reciprocal awareness into the area of human action, and from the meeting ot those energies a mutual "harmonic" is derived. This is generally in terms which can only be appreciated by a high level of human awareness, usually as a sense of acknowledgement that cannot be put into mere words. We do not get our answers in actual words, but as inner certainties quite apart from intellectual or rational sources of self-supply. It is a question of knowing by "feel", rather than by reason.

These inner contacts with higher-than-human types of consciousness, communicating through "Temple conditions," are made at levels very much above our normal range of sensory or verbal interpretaitons. To translate them downwards into appreciable terms of ordinary understanding is not only very difficult, but also unreliable. Very often the best we can do is accept convenient approximations. The physical part of our human anatomy is mainly unaware of such contacts unless sensitized by stresses affecting its well-being such as drugs, prolonged fasting, toxification, ill-health, sleeplessness, or other damaging pressures. Moreover, such stress-stimuli usually result in very confusing and inaccurate impressions needing a great deal of knowledge and experience to evaluate. All things considered, in the light of present human potentials, the wisest course to take is that of simply "reaching up" inside ourselves, then converting our contacts there into more ordinary language by means of adaptive symbology.

Different souls have varied experiences of contacts with inner sources of consciousness. For some, it is like a sudden flash taking a long time to translate afterwards. For others, it could be a combination of sound and vision. Others might simply have a sense of "presence" which nevertheless imparts a satisfactory feeling during its visitation. There could even be an absolutely bland and unresponsive sort of "wall" encountered, that in itself is a contact representing refusal of communication on one side or the other for some definite reason. There are so many types of inner links with suprahuman consciousness, it would be pointless to list them. What really matters is that people should be encouraged to try making their own as an exercise of their spiritual energies.

This is the whole idea of constructing any kind of a Temple. It essentially means calling the Temple into consciousness in and around oneself, then proceeding with meditative or magical procedures according to intention. It takes only a moment to imagine oneself in a Magical Temple striking a deeply reverberating gong, for example. That makes quite an effective exercise by itself. There are many brief yet valuable exercises which only occupy seconds of time, yet serve to maintain the necessary spiritual "charge" of our Temples, providing these are made with sufficient frequency.

From an ideal viewpoint, there is nothing to equal the constant performance of a regular "Office" in a Temple for keeping its "charge" up to maximum efficiency. An Office consists of devotional and liturgical formulae constructed in cyclic style so that a circular continuum of consciousness is operative throughout the whole Time-Space-Event cosmos of a Temple. To understand this, it is only necessary to think of a heavy fly-wheel beautifully balanced on its exact axis. At first it requires much effort to start it revolving very slowly. As one continues, however, the wheel will pick up momentum until eventually it is revolving at a maximum rate relative to the total energy input. Its revolutions can then be utilized for productive purposes. The same principles are valid in Temple practice. The important point is that once the cyclic energy runs at normal working rate it has to be maintained by regular applications of fresh force.

The reality of all this is easily checked by a number of visits to various temples and churches. It will be found that the Roman, Orthodox, and Anglican Christian denominations, which practice regular Offices and rhythmic liturgies, have far more marked and positive "atmospheres". Additionally, those churches are generally open all day for prayer and meditation by individuals. In the case of nonconformist churches, there is more preaching or social activities than active prayer and meditation. Consequently they seldom have very marked atmospheres, often feeling rather vacant and aseptic or "institutional", rather than "alive" and inspirational. A great deal depends on what transpires in the consciousness of their congregations. If this is occupied with secular and commonplace affairs during meetings, then nothing more important is likely to linger around the place when everyone has gone home. There is also the probability that few, if any, of those people spare another thought for their church during their absence. This makes a considerable loss of active energy for its atmosphere. If they had known or cared enough to concentrate on their church and fomulate even a few brief devotions each day, there would be a very definite difference noticed in its "charge" when a full congregation gathered together.

Therefore the basic essentials of building magical Temples in the Western Tradition are these. First, learn how to create them consciously within one's own being according to the system of symbols followed. Next, develop the dynamism of this design by rhythmic and regular ritual usage. Then seek inner contact through this scheme with the higher side of one's own nature, and through that again, communion with superior spiritual orders of living. The entire fabric of Western initiation hangs on this framework, and all inner instructions reaching initiates from senior sources come through some such structure. There are various types and lay-outs of Temples, to be sure, but the fundamental principles apply throughout.

Most young and eager aspirants are chiefly concerned with what to *do* in their Temples, while more experienced members of the Mysteries are mainly occupied with what to *be*. Those looking for active outlets are frequently bothered by an apparent lack of magical material specifically available for practical purposes. Where, they ask wistfully, are all the wonderful written rituals calculated to produce reputedly marvelous results by acting out their scripts? It is difficult indeed to convince enthusiastic hopefuls that such rituals do not exist as specifics at all. Everything depends upon individual and collective ability to link up with inner power-supplies. Some are able to do this with a minimum or absence of words and motions, and others might push through procedures for hours until nearly exhausted. It is not so much the scripting and stage directions of a ritual which give it importance, but the spiritual ability of whoever works with it. The unspoken and imperceptible parts of a genuine occult ritual are commonly of much greater importance than its physically expressed components. Those vital and secret factors are beyond verbal definition. They are only comprehensible to whoever can reach them as inner realities along lines of consciousness rather above or outside average human range.

One customarily begins by practicing very simple ritual workings of the West over and over again in search of deeper and deeper spiritual significance and experience. For instance, lighting a lamp or candle. Externally such an easy act, internally it should be evocative of illumination on spiritual levels. It may mark a position, indicate an intention, or have quite a number of distinct meanings. Whatever the purpose may be, it has to be clearly called into consciousness and focused into bright and burning reality.

The action has to be practiced and practiced, until lighting a candle "sparks off' a state of inner awareness. The magic of the act lies entirely with the inward condition associated with the outward symbol.

It may not seem very interesting or enterprising to keep pounding away at what look like elementary exercises with almost primitive symbols, but Western magical practice is firmly rooted in such self-disciplines. Those who cannot see their significance, or who feel too self-important to bother with them, are unlikely to make much real progress on the Western Inner Way. It takes as much skill and practice at this art as it would for a musician learning to handle tones in composing a sonata, or an author to combine words and ideas into a readable work on some definite topic. A Western magical practitioner is expected to deal with the "Alphabet", "grammar", and other basics of the art, in order to put a full ritual production into practice.

There is no denying that only very marked alterations in Western consciousness can possibly save our spiritual structure from degenerative disintegration. Nevertheless, that fact has to be faced. We need now, as in the past, "Priest-King-Saviors" prepared to devote their lives in the cause of consciousness-changing on behalf of other souls. This happened before on many occasions in our Western history, but perhaps the necessity has never proved so great as at present. Where shall we find our modern magical "Liberators" taking up the challenge to our Tradition on behalf of their bewildered brethren?

7. If We Would Stand

The primary purpose of life in the West is the creation of a uniquely Western soul. Unless this aim is fulfilled to a sufficient degree, our lives have little real meaning. This whole inner structure of our ethos faces the most subtle and dangerous threat to its integrity it has probably had during its entire history. To recognize the reality of our perilous position needs only an intelligent glance at the painfully obvious trends and implications of our current and projected course of "civilization".

Once, history was made by humans out of their own experiences. Now it is being increasingly written by computers in advance of events. These are controlled by concentrated consortiums that could eventually determine the destiny of all mankind. No computer has, or ever will have, the power to injure human souls and spirits except through their own consent and co-operation. At the same time, we are not compelled to seek souls and individual immortality for ourselves. As entities, we are free to "be or not-to-be" as we will. Freedom of such an ultimate sort, however, has never suited the aims of those interested in a caucus-controlled civilization. To hold them in permanent posts of power, they need the continual support of a slave-society willing to work as obliged by the oligarchy.

To run a computerized society for the pleasure and profit of its owners, it is strictly necessary that the human aggregate concerned should be predictable and calculable to the highest possible degree. Unless this can be contrived, the scheme is but partially practical. Hence we have the horrifying picture of humans becoming computer-compliant creatures, processed and conditioned by every scientific resource into conformity with whatever "norm" the "central committee" demands. This is no science-fiction fantasy, but a frightening probability of our very close future.

Within the context of prevailing conditions, the magical branch of our Western Tradition seems best placed as a kind of "Resistance Movement" functioning as freely as possible inside the imposed strictures of society enforced on us by current "civilization". There is nothing new in this. Past history proves that in every generation sincere seekers of spiritual independence have always had to safeguard their integrity through confidential procedures among their special circles. In those days that could be done quite practically, but now things are entirely different. There is no organization of modern times which could not be penetrated by counter-interests, providing sufficient money and talent are forthcoming for that purpose. Therefore, to suppose some type of almost revolutionary "Secret Society of the West" working in opposition to established authoritarianism would be totally unrealistic. Altogether different outlooks have to be adopted if our Inner Tradition is to offer spiritual sanctuary from forces aiming at its ultimate suppression.

Many people thinking along other lines suppose it might be a wonderful scheme to set up some great centralized organization on earth to propagate and push our Western Inner Way into world prominence. They presume that with huge amounts of capital, publicity, and all available modern means of pressuring people, we would not fail to market our "Tradition products" among mankind with maximum effect. Nothing, in fact, would possibly cause it more harm or run it closer to ruin. The entire essence of our Tradition is that each of us must earn and experience inner emancipation with it by his or her own efforts. Finding the linkages leading into our secret circles of spiritual companionship is an indispensible part of our perfection program. We all have to open our inward eyes and look for those leads on our individual accounts.

The only sane course is for modern Western "magicals" to form small, individualized enclaves through which the Tradition will survive. That is the usual way Traditions escape extinction when threatened on mundane levels of life. Like any other living root in the face of approaching winter, they retire gracefully underground and grow stronger while waiting for a more congenial climate on earth. This time, however, we shall have to learn quite new techniques to deal with new dangers.

It probably sounds rather drastic to suggest comparisons between the survival systems of magical Traditionalists and conventional guerilla groups, or "cells", but a resemblance has to be seen because of one common factor. Human experience has proved this the only practical way for ideological minorities to remain active and true to their beliefs while living among a largely indifferent, unsupportive, or antipathetic society. It entails a virtually dual existence or "life within a life". One is openly shared with ordinary fellow mortals. The other is lived either in solitary secrecy, or shared only with a very few souls who can literally be trusted with each other's lives should necessity arise. To some extent there is a parallel with the case of an intelligence agent living under an assumed personality in a foreign country.

A long time ago it was learned that the absolute maximum number of people for forming a magical grouping was twelve humans centering round a single spiritual nucleus. Moreover, they had to be exactly in balance with each other, making a truly proportioned circle in every sense. Unless each member of such an ideal association was precisely the right sort of soul for his particular position therein, the whole affair would be bound to fall apart or produce little but trouble and problems for everyone. The difficulties of assembling a fully functioning Western Magical circle are unbelievable. Therefore, any authentic working groups of the West these days are likely to be small in numbers and exceptionally selective of membership. They would definitely not advertise their relationship or deliberately attract attention to themselves in other than quite ordinary capacities. In other words, they would behave in a professional and responsible manner regarding a common cause they believed of supreme importance to their lives.

Such an attitude is highly commendable. So many people "taking up magic" have an overwhelming urge to "get a little group together" for self-glorification and other equally wrong reasons. This is natural enough, but usually brings unhappiness and difficulties to all involved Relations are artificially assumed with no balanced basis or compatibilities of character, to say nothing about quite usual rules of common sense and custom for forming such intimate and important associations. The uncompromising standard which Western magical workers should set themselves these days is that none should come together into mundane circles who cannot already balance their own beings by themselves. Only properly trained and disciplined followers of the Western Inner Way should be allowed to participate in magical circles operating among mankind at this level of life. This might seem a very rigid rule, but it is needed for the sake of security among the most effective (and therefore the least replacable) members of our incarnate magical force.

So where are "beginners" and "catchers up" to obtain the needed experience and training which will bring them to acceptable standards for service in areas affecting our earthly lives? Nowadays, the responsibility for this lies heavily on their own shoulders. Any average adult in our times should have access to all information needed to train themselves in the elements of magic from public libraries and similar sources. When and if souls become ready and are needed for close co-operation in some active circle of Western magical working, they will surely be guided towards it by "inner invisible hands". Even so, the onus of recognizing the validity of that circle remains very much with the souls in question. Mutual acceptance has to come from the deepest inner levels of understanding.

Few people who are "just interested in the occult" ever seem to appreciate how delicately and carefully the dynamism of individual or collective magical circles has to be balanced and maintained before becoming of much value to our Tradition. To keep going properly they need adequate safeguards from inimical influences, just as the works of a watch must be protected from air-borne dirt, or an operating theater from dangerous infections. In the case of magical circles, this means avoidance of human instabilities on one side, and inner equivalents on the other. This could take the lifework of quite a number of people over several incarnations to achieve. Small wonder they will go to so much trouble in safeguarding so valuable a creation of their consciousness. They are prepared to protect it with every possible precaution imaginable.

Our modern security systems mostly derive from old-time Lodge and Temple customs invented purely to guarantee the integrity of their methods and members. All the elaborate recognition codes, passwords, grips, cyphers, challenges, and other cumbersome procedures were employed so that initiates of the Mysteries could practice their beliefs without annoyance or interference. Very often such simple security measures made the difference between life and death. There is nothing like a threat of torture and deprival of the worst kind for making people take maximum care of their conduct and set inner sentinels over every word they utter. When only secrecy may save them from a feared fate, they soon became creatures of extreme caution. Temples and Lodges learned this long ago, and the principles behind their practices extended into military, commercial, and almost every other field of human activity until "Security" is virtually a household word.

An awful lot of rubbish has been written and supposed about "occult secrecy". Many seem to think this means a few privileged people sitting on a mysterious moutain of advantageous information they are deliberately withholding from those they consider unworthy to share such wisdom. It means nothing of the sort. In the main, it signifies little more than the quite normal confidences humans of any close alliance observe together for the sake of common integrity. Like "family secrets", for instance, or intimacies too precious for publication to outsiders. The secrecy observed among trained Traditionalists is generally practiced on two levels, internally and externally. External secrecy would apply to such affairs as identities of members or clues leading to these, locations of meeting places, things done or discussed together, and so forth. Internal secrecy is observed in common concerning matters which should only be shared on purely spiritual levels above the range of words or intellectual arguments. That is to say, things like individual inner experiences and realizations reached in dimensions of awareness much wider than those of material limitations.

This last may be very difficult for "non-magicals" to grasp. They might think quite logically: "If those people really do have remarkable or interesting experiences in themselves, why shouldn't they talk about these together and mention whatever they like?" Those thinking that way have missed the point entirely. Spiritual secrecy is only kept on "ground level" in order to encourage attention away from that point toward inner areas of awareness which could otherwise be missed by exploring consciousness. Put crudely, it might be said: "Don't drag things down to earth which are best climbed up to and lived with on their natural levels." It is entirely a question of values. Which is better for human souls—to try forcing our highest faculties into faulty and abnormal focus on earth, or learn how to live happily while using them in their own appropriate spheres of consciousness? The answer should be obvious. So, by using simple security techniques among themselves as ordinary human, initiates of magical practice are able to share each other's inner lives as those are most fully experienced, on common grounds of spiritual awareness where they will not be interefered with.

This particular point is of much importance nowadays. Everyone knows that electronic "bugging" makes privacy a difficult matter, but there are other ways of invading along inner lines connected with consciousness itself. Thoughts are not exactly so secret as they were. To avoid interception and deliberate distortion of consciousness by antipathetic agencies, quite new procedures have to be worked out and adopted. Though there may always be ways around, over, under, or through any obstacle, those efforts take an enormous consumption of energy from every field of consciousness. Each magical circle has only its limited supply. If a large percentage is needed to operate an effective security system, there will be so much the less for putting to other purposes. Nevertheless, without security measures at all, there would be virtually nothing worth much in the end, anyway.

In former days the religious Orders, which based themselves very greatly on older magical and mystical associations, realized the enormous importance of caution with consciousness. It was largely during early stages of training alone that topics of religion or theology were dealt with in words or direct discussion. The more that initiates actually learned along those lines the less they talked about such subjects and the better they began to live them instead. Eventually they outgrew inclinations to argue or express their beliefs at all, and discovered how to experience inner realities among themselves without need for words whatever. For that reason they instituted "silent periods" during which they might enjoy each other's company through purely inner channels of communion linking in with higher orders of intelligence also. Audibly uttered human language to them had become merely a very common-place means needed on their lowest levels of living. So all they talked about by word of mouth tended to be quite prosaic, formal, amusing, or relatively trivial. In between those extremes they celebrated, sung, and chanted services providing a sonic symbolism conjoining both ends of their existence. Thus they swung round the cycles of consciousness during the course of each day. For them, silence was no unsociable obligation of any kind. To the contrary, it was a warm and welcome opportunity for coming into the most intimate contact with each other's spiritual reality in closest company with Cosmic Consciousness Itself.

Lovers able to find "whole fulfilment" in each other to a point where the softest whispered word would be sheer sacrilege might understand something of this. So will "magicals" with experience of a Westworking circle of companions. They no longer seek true wisdom in the arguments, opinions, or verbiage of others, no matter how clever or convincing it may seem. Instead, they look for enlightenment within themselves, accompanied by trusted and trained friends in the best sense of that word. It is scarcely surprising they are concerned so much with protecting and preserving something which matters most to them within the Tradition they swear to serve with all their spiritual strength.

It is usually difficult for folk, living in countries where apparent "free speech" is normal, to realize the value and importance of spiritual security. If they lived in lands where they were liable to arrest and imprisonment for voicing unpermitted ideas they would learn fast enough. Westerners rarely see precisely why certain governments should stamp so severely on those expressing prohibited beliefs. Why the elaborate and expensive set-up of secret police, surveillance systems, political prisons, asylums, correction centers, and all else employed at state expense, just to prevent what looks like a few little people talking about their particular ideas. In our eyes it often seem like using a jackhammer to crack an eggshell.

From a magical viewpoint, those suppressive measures enforced at such a staggering cost at least prove one pertinent issue. The establishments concerned are admitting to the whole world that they realize and fear the inherent power and possibilities of any ideology connected to the liberation of public consciousness. To operate inner activities under such restrictive conditions would require a most efficient sort of spiritual security.

On the opposite side of the picture, establishments seeming to encourage free speech and "permissiveness" use much more intelligent methods of opposing movements of magical consciousness which might stir some of the populace to peer higher than TV programs for truth. So far as they are able, they would like all magical enthusiasts out in the open, preferably with as much publicity as possible. They would encourage every crackpot and eccentric to indulge in the wildest and silliest antics imaginable, dressed in the weirdest costumes while performing every variety of inane absurdities. By the time professional journalists had finished their embellished accounts of those events, there would be little left to invite either respect or confidence in realities misrepresented so blatantly. What effect, for example, does it have on millions of viewers, watching some carefully chosen "witch" or asserted occut personality skilfully "interviewed" on TV in such a scientific way that a calculated impression of inferiority is somehow planted in people's minds. In other words, all resources of mass-media and psychological warfare combined are used to devalue, discredit, and make nonsense of our Inner Tradition in the eyes of those it seeks to serve.

If both types of established governments are expending such efforts to negate the inner linkages of our living Tradition, this alone should be sufficient to show their true significance. It ought also to convince those thinking of serious service in the cause of this Tradition how carefully they will have to adjust their lives in order to serve and survive simultaneously.

Apart from these considerations, there is an extremely good psychological reason for the careful cultivation of "magical secrecy". This is to help develop within onself a very special "chamber of consciousness" in which one's own highest abilities of awareness are able to hold some kind of communion with Divine

Intelligence. By excluding all else except an awareness of "I- ness" and "That-ness", a conscious linkage between individuals and the Universal Spirit of Life becomes possible. For a human being, this is a very difficult process, because it calls for expert control of consciousness which is only possible after prolonged practice. One begins by holding concepts securely for the sake of their significance apart from all else in existence. This means keeping them secret in the sense of not allowing them to come in contact with whatever would depreciate their value to their holder. It is instinctive in most people to talk least about what they value most, and this is the principle which applies in spiritual security. All the ceremonies, customs, and "secrets" confided to candidates at initiations are simply symbolic aids for developing an essential inner faculty towards its highest potential. The whole idea itself is symbolized by the "Empty Room", or secret space inside oneself wherein spirit contacts spirit directly. This "Empty Room" is supposed to be the only place one utters one's own Magical Name aloud.

Secrecy and mystery are such an essential part of magic that without correct employment of those elements it would scarcely work to any effective extent. Everything depends on right usage, and this of course depends upon the understanding and capability of the users. Sadly enough, a lot of "occult concerns" only introduce an element of mystery to attract suckers, while others treat it as a screen for extremely dubious activities or downright illegal behavior. This always poses a serious dilemma for would-be entrants. Faced with a curtain of mystery, they must determine whether or not it might be worth penetrating. That of itself is a test of their inner perspicacity. Though it is impossible to lay down hard and fast rules, mysteries concealing sucker-traps are usually accompanied by specious promises of advantage, while more sinister affairs are likely to look for blackmailing holds on prospective members. In each case, the prospect is presented with a mystery which guardians offer to lift for him in return for some consideration. Therein lies the catch. Where genuine spiritual veracities are apparently concealed behind a masking mystery, no initiate of such a system would offer to raise a corner of it for any approaching enquirer. The sole reason for this is because all who would enter the precincts of the Western Inner Way have to penetrate the mysteries entirely by their own efforts. Nobody can clear a pathway through that protection for anyone else, because it consists of an obscurity in and peculiar to each individual. Associates can only encourage, advise, or offer spiritual support.

Maybe the message of an initiated member of our Western Way to some sincere soul seeking fellowship by means of its Mysteries might run something like this:

"Mysteries are metaphors made by man to carry his consciousness closer to that of Cosmos Itself. They are spiritual symbols through which we try to speak the Language of Life. You have made yours as we have made ours. We are not here to explain, expound, or judge anyone's mysteries, but to live out what we are making of ours. All we can do for you is show you how we believe you might do as much for yourself. Everything else lies in your own hands. If that is acceptable to you, then you are welcome to work with us in a spirit of friendship. If not—then go which other way you will."

Only the utmost determination and genuine dedication to our Inner Way of the West can possibly carry it even so far as the next century. Ours has never been a comfortable, easy, and unopposed Tradition to follow. It has always called for indomitable courage in the face of opposition, and unbreakable faith in the principles of individual spiritual freedom, and a spirit of sacrifice willing to keep our Inner Pathways toward Perfection clear at almost any personal cost. Nothing but the finest qualities of character will be equal to the demands made on Western Initiates during the times ahead of us. That has ever been the meaning of our Western Tradition.

Whether the Tradition of the West lives or dies in this world will be determined by whatever faithful few care enough about it to give so that it may live.

No "Great Avatars" are likely to land on this earth in any immediately appreciable form. There will be no incredible "Masters", "Teachers", or fantastic figureheads to lead us out of the murk we have made ourselves. Whatever we need to help us must either be brought through ourselves, or else we go without it until we learn how. In the end, our Inner Tradition has to be carried along by quite ordinary human beings who become conscious of their extraordinary responsibility. Yet never for one second should it be supposed that "the cause is everything and the individuals nothing". Our cause in the Western Tradition *is* individualism. Collectively we have all to help each other BE OUR SELVES.

For the future, our Inner Tradition is best bound up with the work of individuals and extremely select but dependable nuclear groupings, all capable of independent functioning, while linked together through inner channels of consciousness beyond reach of antipathetic influences. The broadest outline of effort within those circles would be roughly:

A. Cognizance of essentials from our past, and preservation of these in practical forms for the future.

B. Interpretation of the spirit behind our Tradition into terms of present potency, and actually living in accordance with these findings.

C. Conceiving and contributing advances of consciousness intended to help ourselves and fellow humans make even the slightest steps ahead along our Inner Paths.

D. Maintaining, modernizing, and projecting the principles of our Tradition so that it continues as a living force in this world. It can then lead its followers towards that truth within themselves enabling each soul to transform itself, becoming an Eternal Entity, ultimately attaining PERFECT PEACE PROFOUND.

Within a perimeter of that magnitude, we can cheerfully consecrate our circles and set up stations for making what magic we may in a constantly current Western manner.

There is one extremely important consideration. Any group assocations on earth level arising out of those Inner necessities should ideally be of a spontaneous, mutually attractive nature. That is to say, people concerned ought to be guided into each other's human company by inner and instinctive leadings instead of looking for some already formed and materially based organizations to join. The reason for this is that no matter how good and noble earth-based occult organizations may mean to be in the first place, they cannot altogether avoid degrees of infiltration and interference. Free and fluid groupings flowing through the structure of Western culture is undoubtedly the best way of keeping our Inner Tradition alive and active in our times. Our symbol of the West is water, after all, and if we sanctify this into the Blessed Blood borne by the "Grail," that should provide enough ideas to inspire couses of action for an indefinite period ahead.

There is an old analogy of every living creature represented as being some essential part of a unified Whole Divine Life, or "Cosmic Corpus". Within that fictional framework, it was customary to consider the average members of mankind as flesh or sinews, while the "chosen" or highly developed elite entered the actual bloodstream. This was, and yet is, the inner meaning of our Eucharistic Sacrament. The idea was that if an Almighty God "ate us up", and incorporated us immortally into Its Being, we should become equivalent to Its flesh and blood. Therefore, if we partook of flesh and blood, or bread and wine as the symbols thereof, in the Name of that God, this proved our willingness to be so consumed and continued in the Consciousness of Cosmos.

Which brings us back (as most things always will) to the Grail workings of the West. Here we see the mysterious Grail in quite a new light. It becomes in fact those who are worthy of becoming both the metaphorical and mystical "Divine Blood" within the Western Inner Tradition. We must remember that traditionally "Blood" means not only a bearer of Life within a body, but also the carrier of an entire genesis, and therefore intrinsically all future potential and ultimate ends of evolution. This is what the "Holy Grail" really means for the West—that which is "in our blood" for the purpose of bearing us towards Godhood.

Here, beyond any possible doubt, is the "Great Work of the West." Under the symbology of the Grail, our whole "bloodstream of Life" has to be circulated throughout our structure so that we can actually *live* as vital and important beings belonging to ourselves and each other in a Single Spirit. Somehow that Spirit in our blood has to be stirred and set flowing through the choked channels of consciousness which should be supplying us all with means and motives for moving our mentalities toward higher levels of living than those so many are accepting as inevitable.

8. "The More It Changes, the More It Stays the Same

A Tradition should grow naturally out of itself like any other form of life. Whatever stops growing and developing is then dead and best buried for fertilizer of fresh and promising issues. To that extent our Tradition is like a tree. Its roots remain deep beneath surface levels of life, its stem and main branches have arisen within us, while its leaves and fruits are seasonally subject to climatic changes and conditions. Looking at the Tree of Life pattern, we should note that its three Pillars are sometimes equated with three basic principles of Existence. Force and Form are on the outside. Equilibriating fundamentals constitute the all-important Middle Pillar. Forces and Forms are changables, but Fundamentals are the axis-points, in relation to which any alterations are made.

To keep a Tradition healthy, it is necessary to maintain its "leaf and fruit" equivalents in appropriate conditions of change while its fixed fundamentals supply its inner needs from spiritual sources beyond our immediate grasp. Be it always understood, however, that no alteration should ever be made purely for the sake of change itself. Such changes should be made because of fluctuating influences within what could be called the "Cosmic climate" we live in. Just as there are standard seasonal flux taking place, so are there spiritual tides and seasons with many variations of rate and effect. Some changes need centuries of our time to occur, others take only seconds. Some affect the destinies of entire races and nations, and others only apply to individuals. All are interrelated through deepest levels of Life. We have to adapt with them as best we may from one incarnation to another, while striving to modify them beneficially during our existence. That is where Tradition can be so valuable. Through its means, we can impress alterations into its spiritual substructure which are bound to bring eventual benefits.

The old idea of living within a Tradition meant whatever of value was put into it during a lifetime not only resulted in useful or happy excarnate experience, but also might provide somewhat better conditions for subsequent rebirth. This is comparable to "keeping it in the family". If all its members made what contributions they could then everyone included should theoretically be better off with every birth, so long as the Tradition were kept alive through the generations. This is fundamentally true enough, though of course membership has enlarged proportionately through many incarnations. At the same time, full membership of a Tradition must be consciously claimed and intentionally maintained. It is not enough to be born within a Tradition. There has to be active participation and involvement with its spiritual implications.

In times past, most people instinctively knew or recognized the Tradition they belonged with because it was essentially a "family, friends, and neighbors" affair. None of it came from books. Everything emerged from what others passed on by word or example which resulted in individual reactions with all this by succeeding generations. Woven in among that stream of consciousness were the subtle influences of non-incarnate intelligences attempting to guide human evolution toward higher and finer levels of living. A Tradition thus supplied humans not only with a sense of "What I have been before this", but a complementary sense of "What I am going to be afterwards." It extended existence on both sides of incarnation. How are modern humans to obtain such a sense of identity without feeling some Inner Tradition behind and before their transient physical foci?

They are unlikely to obtain very much from families and friends, with rare exceptions. Official sources, such as schools and

Churches, are necessarily bound to the socio-political dictates of an anonymous autocracy. Modern Westerners are not encouraged to believe in or hope for individual spiritual liberty and evolution into immortal identity. Their whole conditioning and mind-manipulation inclines them to accept life from very low levels. More and more, mass-mankind tends to identify with its machines and materialistic environments. Little by little they are becoming like "battery-bred" farm animals confined to a production line taking them only from birth to death for the profit of controllers and owners. Perhaps most shocking of all, they enjoy and delight in an enslavement providing them with creature comforts and sensory satisfactions in exchange for their energies of existence. Whether they will ever break away from this bondage is for history to show. The fact remains that it imposes a heavy constraint on Western consciousness during the present epoch which seems unlikely to lesson very much in the foreseeable future.

The Western Way began because of a spiritual need for individuation which was being opposed and thwarted by controllers determined to impose their own interests upon all humans. Our Inner Way commenced as what would nowadays be called a "Liberation Movement", and fundamentally stands for exactly the same principles in our times as it did then. There is this difference. We can no longer move away from menace on the physical plane.

We have to face working the Western Way within antagonistic conditions and confusing circumstances. Like Luther, we are being driven into positions when we must sooner or later say the words that gave him fame as an antagonist of corruption within an Established Church: "Here stand I. I can do no other." It could scarcely be coincidental that the device on Luther's seal was a combination of Rose, Cross, and Heart. What he professed openly was certainly connected with beliefs and outlooks held secretly among Temples and Lodges operating in Europe at that period.

So here we now have to stand, wherever we happen to be, and follow our ancient Faith in a modern manner since we also can do no other. Interpretations of that Faith may vary, but basically it goes back to the origins of our Tradition itself. Defining articles of any Faith is always a most difficult matter, yet in the very broadest of terms a Westen esotericist of any branch might agree with these wide definitions:

1.   The inherent Life-motive of every living soul should be to evolve and individuate itself into an ultimate integer of our Universal Entity.

2.   Achievement of such an attainment is possible through voluntary sacrifice of low-level self-life for the sake of spiritual Selfhood. Such sacrifice is made through and by the principles of "priesthood" and "kingship" in each individual. Properly understood, this is the "Holy Grail" of our Western Way.

3.   Though each individual is ultimately responsible for its own salvation, we are all obliged to help each other in a mutual perfection process insofar as may be consistent with individuation needs and procedures.

4.   We have to recognize, and discover how to work with the assistance of other life-orders beyond our conditions of embodiment, which are most closely concerned with our chosen Inner Way of developing toward Divinity.

5.   We have to learn and understand the use of our inherited cultural and special spiritual symbology, whereby conscious communication and exchanges of energy become possible between our human ends of entity and those higher levels of living we aim to exist in ourselves eventually.

6.   We are here to pick up genetic links from our past we made as power-points for our perfection-program modify these as and if now necessary, then follow this "Western Line of Light" forward toward the Truth we seek.

7.   We should respect and recognize the Spirit of Life in all our fellow creatures whether human or otherwise, acting towards them as agents of that same Spirit in ourselves.

Though there could be many other points put forward, these few should serve as a fair background of belief behind our esoteric endeavors. Projected into modern "humanitarian" terms, they are an acknowledgement that "people", in the sense of being living souls, are far more important than productions, profits, politics, or any artificial abstractions and materialistic substitutes. Summed up to a single succinct point, we are here to help each other become as the Divine Intention within us wills.

It is important that the study and practice of the Western Inner Tradition should not be thought of as merely interesting rambles into the past. To the contrary, as all our past spiritual streams condense in the present, we should be impressing our modern adaptations of its meaning. Our myths and legends have to be interpreted in terms of today, and our magic likewise cast into circles of current consciousness. That is a tremendous and most serious responsibility for everyone involved. It is only possible if the right people are really prepared to spend whole incarnations in such work, and pass on what they have done to their spiritual heirs for further development. That much is obvious. What is not so readily appreciated is exactly how such a process takes place.

In old times, it was a straightforward matter of passing links to the Tradition directly from parent to child. In some cases fathers passed these to sons and mothers to daughters, sometimes it was the opposite. Often responsibilities were mixed, fathers initiating children into certain parts of a Tradition, and mothers taking other branches. Where there was usually a high mortality among warrior males, a Tradition might necessarily be mostly transmitted through the females. The point is that youngsters freely accepted whatever they received that way, because there were no other means of reception. Consequently, the trans-mission of a Tradition formed a fairly clean line of descent.

Nowadays, the picture is utterly altered. There are very few parents capable of passing much except propaganda-formed ideas to their children, and those children themselves are literally bombarded from all directions with suggestions and influences emanating from politico-commercial sources very much at variance with the spirit inspiring our basic traditional beliefs. Not only that, a virtual "anti-culture" has become established which is entirely opposed to Traditional themes of thought. In the middle of all this muddle, how can any child really feel certain what its Inner belongings are? How on earth can any recent arrival to Western incarnation possibly know what *is* of our Tradition, and what *is not?*

There is really but one practical course for promotors of our Tradition to take. Let out into public areas an adequate supply of external "leads" which, if recognized and followed up with sufficient interest, will steadily guide people into more selective circles. Eventually close and confidential contact can be made with whoever has had the perception and patience to "enquire within." Those "lead-ins" could consist of almost anything. A song with "key phrases" in it for instance. A book with a special passage thrown in among seemingly casual conversation. A picture, or even a poster that symbolically stimulated an inner sense of "belonging with" something that lies far, far behind the presented surface. Absolutely any form encountered objectively in our whole cultural field which is specially designed to attract the attention of "natural" fellow Traditionalists, and encourage them to look longer and deeper in search of the inner reality whose flickering reflection they saw for a split second.

"Lead-ins" of this kind are actually to be found almost everywhere. They have different meanings and connections which appeal to wide varieties of people, but in the main they all carry the same message: "There is something in and behind me which concerns your own immortal identity. Seek this if you will." It is incredible how that vital intimation can be connected to apparently absurd or trivial things in common usage. Perhaps the design of a dress, the feel of materials, the scent of something, the shape of an artifact. Modern magical symbols abound in all directions. It is only a matter of finding what and which unlocks the inner awareness of whom.

The idea of this diversity is that, with such a widespread reach, souls with a spark of the Western Tradition in them will pick up needed threads and clues. How do these links get into circulation? Most often through inner influences affecting the consciousness of those responsible for materializing them. This may take place purely on subconscious levels. But the ultimate issue is that something observable and cognizable by ordinary humans emerges which carries a specific suggestive charge connecting with the spirit of our Tradition.

Suppose, for example, a local potter makes a number of artifacts. He feels inspired to include some motif which is in fact a definite symbol rooted in our Tradition. The potter may simply like the design without being consciously aware of any reason. His productions are bought by a large number of people. Most of these will treat them as artwork only. Here and there, however, the symbolic design will act as a key which unlocks a number of vital determinants in some soul, because that design corresponds with an inner perceptual pattern. Nothing very marked is likely to happen at first, but initial inner releases can lead to considerable advances of consiousness later. Impulses to enquire along certain lines. An aroused curiosity and interest in spiritual subjects.

Altered outlooks in living. These may manifest in small ways at first, but they are important to a human soul.

By this time an ordinary person might well be forgiven for saying: "What on earth is the need for all this dissemination and concealment of clues? Why not simply say our Western Tradition is this, this, and that, so take it or leave it. Why mess around with make-believe and mystery?" If only life *could* be that straight-forward! None would be happier than those trying to maintain the truths of our Inner Way. Perhaps the saddest truth to admit is that the spiritual structure of our Tradition cannot be openly manifested among mankind under the conditions of civilization prevailing on this planet. Our "Grail" has perforce to "hide" for the sake of our souls' survival. If our energies are engaged on material levels in a literal life-or-death struggle to exist as independent entities, we shall need to keep our Inner reserves in safe and secret places. The obvious course to take at present is a strategic one.

Intelligent Western Traditionalists will realize that our immediate way ahead has to be undertaken with considerable caution and capability. There is nothing to be gained by open ideological conflict with established authorities. The thing to do is concentrate on maintaining contact with our appointed "Inner Guardians", while mediating their influence into current streams of consciousness which may help fellow humans find whatever they are seeking within themselves. Most of mankind needs this type of liberating magic more than any other miracle. This is the work that modern Western magi should be mainly concerned with.

In order to appreciate this problem more deeply, it might be good to examine some of the magical attempts made in earlier times and contrast these with recent revivals. Even the convo-luted grimoires of the Middle Ages afford inferential evidence of humans attempting to establish individual relationships with spiritual agencies for independent reasons. Granted the motiva-tions were usually bad and the methods most impractical. Nevertheless, the human need for expressing some kind of inner identity and experiencing the existence of other than mundane orders of life is very genuine indeed.

Think once more of the old-fashioned idea of a magician standing in a circle invoking some spiritual creature into manifest form within a smaller circle traced outside the magician's stronghold. This shows a pattern of enforcing inner entities down to our lower levels of consciousness so as to deal with them from that standpoint. Even a medieval magician seldom supposed very advanced types of entity would be greatly interested in maintaining communication with mankind under those conditions. But then, they were not much concerned with contacting higher orders of life than their own. Their ambition was meeting non-incarnates even lower than themselves which would gratify their importunate demands and generally act as agents for appeasing the worst side of human nature in return for energies which could have been used to improve our inner evolution. This was then called "selling a soul to the Devil."

Contrast this with the modern magical theory. One sets up an effective self-circle for the specific purpose of raising consciousness to a point where it is capable of contacting superior spiritual entities on their natural levels, communicating directly, removed from materialistic perspectives. Put in simple phraseology, instead of dragging spiritual beings down to our human levels of living, we are learning how to lift ourselves up toward their states of existence and even think to some extent as they do. That is modern magic at its best.

Not only do the older magical rituals need contemporary reconstruction, but new developments should emerge from them and open up fresh inner fields of exploration. Our experience in ritual psycho-dramatics should richen and ripen with successive generations until there is something very splendid and wonderful to be worked with in this world. Regrettably this has not been the case. Far from keeeping up advances in this important field, our standards have fallen so low that many, mainly young people, are still trapped in a maze of medieval magic. Considering our resources, the lack of adequate ritualistic facilities is nothing less than deplorable. This is indeed another modern responsibility for dedicated Western Inner Traditionalists to accept and acquit themselves of.

The openings and opportunities for this kind of work are almost countless, and only the barest beginnings are yet being made. There is virtually limitless scope for those specialist souls with a gift for constructing magical rituals which can consistently produce specific spiritual reactions among participants. Not only is the whole range of human feeling available, but also extensions of these we have yet to reach in time to come. The same is true intellectually. We are very far indeed from maximum brilliance in this direction. Therefore all types of magical ritual which encourage and facilitate our inner evolution beyond present average points of arrival, should be more than welcome within our Western Way.

There are neglected and ill-served areas of the human psyche causing us a lot of quite unnecessary trouble which could well be straightened out and normalized by correct channeling through ritual. Take, for instance, a subconscious resentment against a personified Deity, or "Life Itself", which builds up slowly in the souls of so many people. This results in a serious imbalance unless there is some way of neutralizing or releasing the inner pressures so accumulated.

This mounting feeling that "Life is against me" is probably one of our most serious problems, especially in modern times when such a statement seems so obviously factual. People trying to live honest, hardworking, and maybe high-principled lives are apt to abandon ideals when they see ill-motivated opportunists wallowing in wealth, luxury, and indolence while holding the highest social and political positions. With no outlet or adequate provisions for neutralizing this inner pressure, it cannot do much else than become what was once termed a "canker in the soul". Once this gets a firm grip, it is bound to become a focus for damaging forces having a bad effect throughout the entire organism. Though effects may vary, the general result is detrimental. This should be realized by common-sense alone.

Centuries back, people under this same type of pressure would have blamed their Gods for these misfortunes, and demonstrated their disappointment in Divinity with a cathartic commotion in their temples. They would literally have confronted statues or representations of their divinities and acted out their pent-up inner feelings in no uncertain fashion. Excitable individuals might rage away at their Gods in the crudest fashion, pouring forth torrents of abuse, reproaches, and every kind of condemnation. Others might simply give vent to a sense of feeling hurt and neglected, reminding the Deity that better treatment was expected from so high an Entity. However those people acted, they released their tensions through ritualized activities, got an enormous amount of spiritual poison out of their systems, and felt considerably relieved and better for the practice. More important- ly, they may have set currents of consciousness in action which might inititate some mitigating or alleviating influence to work with ills complained of.

Later, as might be expected, powerfully established systems of religion strongly discouraged any form of overt reproach or reproval directed against official concepts of Divinity. That seemed too much like criticism of the ruling elite, which might have stirred up enough discontent to cause civil troubles among disgruntled sections of the populace. The Judaeo-Christian system altered its originally liberative theme and instituted a Divinity identifying with ecclesiastical and civil authority. This meant that the wretched rank and file of membership had no means of expressing resentment. No matter how badly they fared in this world, they were commanded to accept such treatment as being the "Will of God", who would ultimately reward them in Heaven for their uncomplaining sufferings on earth. They were even supposed to thank the same God and His benevolent Church for having them burned alive to save the remnants of their immortal souls. Is it any wonder that deep and implacable hatreds of Gods and Churches alike became idelibly imprinted into human souls.

The same is true today. How is anyone to formulate and express deeply seated and destructive resentment against social and other injustices of life presided over at a very remote distance by an allegedly beneficent Deity? Short of terrorism and atheism, which have nothing but evil effects everywhere, there appear to be no recognizable methods of showing active disapproval of Divinity as misinterpreted by Mankind. So, deeply continued hurts and hates are genetically transferred from one lifetime to another, while on and on goes the bitter story of human inner resistance against whatever makes earth-life miserable and unhappy.

This is where skilled ritualists can provide very practical help by working out ways of releasing and neutralizing those deadly repressed resentments and feelings in human beings which will channel the liberated energy into useful and beneficial pathways. It is true that some psychiatric specialists have been experiment- ing along such lines for quite a while, though with very erratic and uncertain results. Patients have been encouraged to scream their heads off, savagely attack dummy figures representing their pet hates, vomit heartily, or express their loathing of life in various other acts of arranged violence. That may indeed afford temporary relief from their tensions, like masturbation does, but it is no long term or satisfactory answer to their problems, because there has been no proper redirection of expended energy into corrective channels. Discovering some ideal means of dealing with this difficult question is surely a priority task for modern Western esotericists.

There is enough to be done for our Tradition on purely scholastic lines to keep a small army of specialists occupied for some years yet. What we really need most are far fewer rehashers, and many more original thinkers opening up greater opportunities for adventurous followers. Why else should we bother at all with past magical practice except to help us make a good flexible springboard for taking present day trial trips toward Inner spiritual Space. Nevertheless, the greatest caution will always be needed to guide even the most imspired guesses.

For instance, an important point often overlooked in studies of the Western Tradition is that its inner wisdom can degenerate as well as appreciate. Formerly clear-cut and valuable processes of consciousness may slide slowly down until they reach bare survival level for centuries as superstitions and customs continued without much meaning or apparent significance. Nevertheless, as long as they remain in some kind of circulation, much of their former force can be recovered by intuitive investigators. We owe our Peasant section of the Tradition a considerable debt for preserving a lot of "lost" knowledge in this way through folk-tales and other means. A tremendous amount of this has been turned up in recent times, but here are a couple of examples which are probably not so well known.

The first is the practice of sticking pins in a wax image to cause equivalent injuries to whoever the image represented. Although transference of energy by intention projected through symbolism is a fundamental of magical practice all over the world, the wax image custom appears to derive from the ancient art of acupuncture as developed by the Chinese. In teaching the art they employed fairly large models of a human body made of wax and covered with markings in red and black to indicate all vital points for insertion of needles. Pupils had to practice and practice with these models for a very long time before being allowed to treat an actual patient. They were also shown in particular which zones to avoid, because it was believed that wrong placement of needles could cause disease and death. Pupils had to satisfy examiners that they realized the risks run and would never endanger their patients' lives intentionally by needling any fatal positions on a living body.

Little by little this general idea leaked into misunderstanding minds utterly unable to deal with such concepts and it deteriorated into a supposition that humans could be hurt or killed by pushing pins into representative images made of wax. Now and again, of course, engendered currents of hate-tuned consciousness did in fact damage whoever they were aimed at, providing suitable linkage was established. The doll itself was no more than a focal point to help concentrate the required inner power. Eventually the whole practice was devalued by Westerners until it sank down to "witchcraft" levels, losing almost all of its original meanings.

Possibly a modern Western attempt to retrieve this situation is the theory of "Radionics". A spot of blood or body secretion from the individual to be treated is related with and electronic tuning circuit supposed to transmit "healing currents" towards the patients wherever they happen to be physically. Some operators of this system believe it helps if they also concentrate on a photograph or picture of the person in question. So do some "spiritual healers" who like to have a little physical linkage with their distant objectives through a picture, lock of hair, or almost any small intimate object. Our "wax image" ideas have improved somewhat over the centuries, and perhaps may reach an altogether higher and much more accurate inner means of helping fellow humans with "unseen hands".

Another recondite illustration of old ideas gone wrong through misinterpretration in the West is the sad downfall of flagellation into sheer sadism and stupid cruelty. At one time in certain initiated circles mainly in Egypt, it was a highly skilled psychological and therapeutic art. Very loosely, it consisted of expert application of long thin rods mostly to the spinal area with extremely precise pressures and rhythms. This stimulated or depressed nerve centres in such a way as to affect consciousness by calculated degrees in specific directions. The strokes delivered called for a practiced and long-trained operator. The practitioner had to know where to hit with his stimulators and also for how long, with what frequency. In general, the blows were usualy quite light, flicking more than flogging. Altogether the entire exercise was intended to be scientifically beneficial.

Quite a number of effects were noted. One was that the subject's consciousness became stimulated and intensified to a marked degree. Eventually, the treatment extended to the fields of mental disorders, and in the right hands could improve conditions of insanity. Then, too, there seemed to be some good physical side effects in amelioration of illness, especially rheumatic and arthritic pains. The mystical value of the practice was principally during preparatory phases of initiation procedures. Properly worked, it was intended to help the candidate reach a suitable stage of consciousness for appreciating part of the proceedings as it should be experienced. With a well-trained operator and the candidate in the right frame of mind to start with, the entire operation could be a rapid and efficient affair.

This became one of the most misused malpractices. From scientific stimulation it soon down-graded to brutal floggings and ill-treatment of often helpless humans. Victims were told they had to stand so many lashes as a condition of initiation in order to test their endurance or expiate guilt. Any kind of excuse served for sadistic superiors to inflict pain and humiliation on others. As late as the eighteenth century, defenceless lunatics were subjected to vicious beatings all over their bodies. This was believed to improve their behavior, even though there was no evidence it did any such thing. Schoolchildren were lashed for stupidity. A beating was thought to brighten their brains. Monks and nuns flogged themselves with "disciplines" till their backs were pouring with blood. They thought this would stimulate spiritual feelings, "beat the Devil out of them", bring them credit for vicarious suffering on behalf of others, soften the wrath of the Almighty, and entitle them to a great share of happiness in heaven because of what they had endured on earth. No wonder most old-time "Guardians of the Mysteries" tried to keep details of their procedures secret. They realized only too well how these would be degraded and desecrated if they reached unworthy minds and hands.

So when encountering interesting fragments of the Western Inner Tradition, it is always well to wonder what proportion of them may have descended from nobler ancestry and whether they should be reconstituted in our times for any pertinent purpose. On one hand it seems useless continuing with anything having little or no relevence nowadays, yet on the other, we cannot afford to lose all touch with once valid concepts. Times have a habit of turning full circle after very prolonged periods, and we may eventually need very old things for very new reasons. For instance, with all our vaunted technology, we still dare not neglect our knowledge of primitive skills which could be needed yet to save the remnants of our civilization after it crashes.

Luckily, this is being realized in some quarters, and adventurous young people are being encouraged to take training courses in wilderness living and survival techniques. Once learned these are never forgotten, and are passed down along the line of their children. Those are the people who will be needed to come forward in the event of a civilization collapse, to start building a new world out of the ruins. Specialists who know how to manipulate markets and make millions would be utterly worthless then. Anyone knowing how to catch and cook food or construct sound shelters for families would be beyond price. Once more our young Sacred Kings would lay down their lives for the sake of tribal survival and our Traditional pattern of living continues its course through another cycle.

No matter how marvelous modern man ever becomes, we will always be entirely dependent in this world upon basic supplies of food, fuel, and fitments. Without these we cannot continue our current courses and would have to fall back upon previous levels of living. That is where Tradition would prove its inestimable value by connecting up our consciousness with points on our preplodded Paths we either missed at the time or paid no attention to because we were aiming elsewhere. There is a great deal in our past we could have done or might have accomplished had we not been coming our present way. Should circumstances ever drive us back on our tracks, and we had to re-investigate undeveloped past potentials, awakened intuitions aroused through our Inner Tradition would start leading us along fresh and quite probably better lines of living altogether.

It is the magical branch of our Tradition which mostly maintains those conscious inner linkages with other and higher orders of living intelligence. Religion may be an officially approved agency for contact with superior spiritual authorities, but how many humans really accept this in their hearts? Certainly not those who control our socio-commercial structure through the course of civilization. They discovered long ago that organized religion was a very practical means of mass-management if its human directions were offered a large enough percentage, and so it has been ever since. Magically motivated individuals are no more immune from pecuniary pressures than anyone else, but they are usually wider awake to inner influences and tend to value their initiated identities considerably above average market prices of human souls.

On the whole, it is a simple question of "occult economics". Most magically awakened individuals feel they have worked long and hard for many incarnations to achieve whatever degree of spiritual independence they may have reached. This has cost them a great deal in terms of experience, suffering, and human endurance through circumstances of all conceivable kinds. To risk the results of all this effort for the sake of ephemeral earthly offers would be unthinkable. In material terms, it would be tantamount to a prosperous person putting the whole of his wealth into a single stockholding which would make him a millionaire for a few weeks, then plunge him into a state of poverty ruining the rest of his life. Some souls might be insane enough to do just that. Medieval magicians were reputed to offer their souls for seven years of luxury. There is nothing to show how many, if even one, managed to sell themselves for that much.

Whoever attempts to live magically must also accept its obligations and pains. The most to hope for is that these will come in mild installments at a reasonable and bearable rate! In bygone times, initiatory Temple preceptors tried their best to make this evident and unmistakable to enthusiastic entrants. These were repeatedly warned and reminded in every possible way that inner progress had to be paid for in full. Everything was done to discourage them from going ahead on their Paths unless and until they realized the tremendous responsibilities entailed.

Today, the same strictures apply, though it seems a pity that the facts of inner life are seldom made uncompromisingly clear for those who try and awaken to them. It might be a very good thing if modern exponents of our Tradition leaned with a little harder emphasis on the duties and obligations which Life itself lays heavily on the shoulders of those who think themselves suitable to serve its cause. Let any such soul be forced to face and acknowledge his own limitations by careful trials and tests to show him his true capacity and capabilities. Only when he has fully realized and understood exactly how he stands on his Inner Path, should he be allowed to take consciously self-sacrificial steps along it.

More and more, the potential and projective power of pure consciousness is becoming apparent among mankind. Sooner or later, quite ordinary folk are going to open themselves up from inside and find out just what they can do with consciousness. Whether they will do the right or wrong things remains to be seen. More than a great deal depends on how seminal streams of consciousness have already been handled by magically initiated souls somewhat ahead of mainstream mankind. Those specialists are supposed to process and re-project the currents of consciousness so that they become easier and better for others to pick up and deal with. Modern magi must be the mediators and modifiers of liberative Inner Illumination so that we may best be led by Light in the West.

Virtually everyone taking even the least conscious part in this program becomes ipso facto a member of what could be called the Magical Order of the Western Way. This is a strangely secret society with a membership mostly unknown to each other, yet operating through a common consciousness conjoined on inner levels. This Order has no organization evident on earth, nobody apparently in authority, no recognizable rules and no distinguishable marks of identification. In fact, there is not even any solid proof of its existence. Ordinary investigators would discover nothing but an uncertain number of individuals behaving as if they were motivated by unusual beliefs quite beyond verification by orthodox academic standards. None but those with exceptionally awakened inner perceptions should suspect the spiritual structure linking all those individual lives together in a common cause they were very willing to serve.

That is the way it will have to be if we are to hold any great hopes for our future. In old Rosicrucian parlance, this was called the "Invisible Government", reputed to be collections of consciousness or "Colleges", linking back to a Divine directorate. This was not meant to indicate something that dictated or decreed our destiny in an arbitrary fashion. The term "College" was used to mean an inwardly available advisory service so that we could learn how to live properly as humans on our pathways to perfection. Whether or not we did so was and still is our own responsibility entirely. If we are interested in saving ourselves, then we must become our own Sacred Kings. Such is the hard, yet at the same time heartening "Message" that modern Mankind must sooner or later accept. Should that be too much for ordinary mortals to comprehend, then their magically enlightened brethren will have to mediate it on their behalf. As usual!

9. What Now?

The magic mankind needs most in any century is one which will direct the drives of our individual and collective consciousness toward higher and finer aims in living. It is painfully obvious in our present era that we must either drastically alter ourselves inwardly, or face very desperate extremities of existence on this planet. We have come to the crunch of "either—or" at last. Either we are prepared to start working in accordance with the "perfecting principle" behind our lives, or we are not. We shall stand or fall on that single point alone.

If we intend to perfect ourselves, then we shall have to admit that higher beings than humans not only exist, but are somehow linked with us along lines of Life leading to their superior states. Moreover, we need to connect our living with theirs by whatever means will influence our consciousness correctly. That is how a Tradition helps us in this world. This is the purpose of its spiritual structure, whether we call it magic, religion, philosophy, or something else. The true value of a Tradition is enabling its members to seek their "Real Identity" on every level of life.

When out of incarnation, human souls tend toward associative circles according to their inherent states of spiritual development. They are not all mixed together as in earth-life, but sorted into natural categories of essential entity. There is nothing stranger in this than separating chemical combinations into specific elements. In the case of human souls, however, it results in states once classified as "Heaven, Hell, and Purgatory." Souls automatically place themselves as they correctly belong for whatever they amount to as individuals. Furthermore, they are most likely to travel along inner tracks laid through Traditionally conditioned consciousness. Eventually, as they reincarnate, there is bound to be an inclination to reflect or recreate those inner experiences in terms of earth-living, except that close contact with other mixed masses of mortals modifies matters considerably.

This is a main advantage in incarnation. It provides a platform for souls in widely different categories of creation to reach and relate with each other under conditions of mutual manifestation. It also allows us opportunities to make much needed modifications and changes in our natures which would otherwise take far more time and trouble through prolonged procedures of purely spiritual advancement. In that sense, our common world forms a very convenient energy-exchange for entities accepting consciousness as a convenient medium of currency. All of us here, whether human, animal, plant, or anything else, have something unique to offer in exchange for necessities only obtainable from other beings.

Occultists in particular should realize that the main reason we reincarnate is because we are not perfect enough to live in better conditions of Cosmos elsewhere. Our chief purpose on this planet is obtaining sufficient stature on all levels of life to get away from it and stay in higher states altogether. So the vast majority of the population will always consist of those souls that are not ready for permanent residence in more evolved states of creation. Strictly speaking, this can never be a perfect world, but we are here to learn how to make one for ourselves in spiritual dimensions. In order to do this, we need influences and inspirations filtering down to us through chains of consciousness connected with those exalted spheres. That means mediation of some sort along the entire line. If all this worked as it should, we would be greatly more advanced than we are at present. Therefore our esoteric experts had best employ themselves finding out the faults of our spiritual systems and, if possible, getting them in good serviceable order again—assuming they were once adequate in the first place.

Our old-time Traditional system was straightforward in a hierarchical way. At the top of its psycho-structure was the Eternal Entity. This consciousness permeated down the scale of "Divine Descent" through a series of mediations, until reaching mankind and lower yet on the Ladder of Life. Keeping close touch with human consciousness and Inner Intelligence alike, our Sacred Kings and Avatars freely offered themselves and their services for the sake of those they loved on earth. Their discarnate function was to maintain such mediatory contact with their folk through channels of communication kept clear by trained specialists eventually called priests. They had to pass this along in modified form to the next class of consciousness, and so on to the lesser end of the human chain. Presumably these last on the list passed on their portions into the animals and plants they tended, and whatever materials, metals, or minerals they came in contact with. So was man-mediated consciousness supposed to cycle its way through our kingdom into others and back to Divinity again bearing beneficial results all around.

A beautiful theory, but one which could only be practiced through the strictest arrangement of stratified society, wherein everyone lived harmoniously together. All the same, it formed a base pattern which still makes a model for Western Magicians to copy while constructing their individual microcosms. We must discover how to become that whole society in each of ourselves. We won't learn this from any printed pages of instructions or any amount of talking done by the most impressive teachers. Modern Westerners have a tendency to rely far more on printing and preaching than they rightly should. Spiritual truths or real "occult secrets" cannot possibly be imparted by such means. They are only transmittable inwardly on direct lines of contact between one consciousness and another. Nor can they be expressed at all on earth-levels except by suggestive symbolism, which may induce individuals to seek inner realities because of glimpses received from outer reflections. In earlier eras this was better understood. None would expect a "Teacher" to give long explanatory lectures and sheaves of secret instructions in writing. Disciples simply came closely around their chosen Mediator, absorbing what they needed from the currents of pure consciousness circulating in that type of magic circle. We very much need to re-learn this method in our times.

It is sad that official formative education seems so inadequate for conceiving or coping with the specific contacts of inner consciousness we humans require for lifting ourselves above material altitudes. Nor might any reliance be placed on conspicuously "way out" characters with tortuous theories, peculiar practices, or other odd customs. In the end it remains the responsibility of unobtrusive Western Traditionalists to make those vital contacts, then re-cycle them through current fields of our common consciousness.

When we come to consider the tides of human thought in general, one strange factor seems apparent. The thinking of millions is seriously influenced by maybe a few thousand minds at most. Those particular thousands are influenced to relative degrees by perhaps a hundred or less comparable sources of consciousness. How many of these again are making the "master concepts"? Lastly, who might be the single mind behind the smallest and most select circle? Is all our incarnate intelligence summed up by one individual living in secure secrecy somewhere with the weight of the world upon him like an archetypal Atlas? However much of a science fiction story this supposition seems, it is impossible to dismiss the idea altogether. Earlier Mystery-systems postulated a "super-soul" of that kind under various titles, the most familiar to us being "LOGOS", or Word.

This Logos-concept is almost self-explanatory. A word is technically a summation of consciousness common to all who share it. The more consciousness concerned, the more significant and important words become. Every individual is thus analogically a Word as expressed by his total awareness. Such is supposed to be symbolized by initiatory "Magical Names." If Cosmos is the creation of an "All-Conceiver", then the summative Name of that Being is the Master-word of total manifestation. Hence the passage: "In the beginning was the Word...," because an initial impulse comparable to the concept of a Word began everything. Hence also the magical importance of "words", which are actually neither written nor spoken human utterances, but condensations of consciousness having sufficient force and meaning to initiate changes along chains of existence extending through many levels of life.

Practitioners of modern Western magic need to become quite literally "Words" of such a sort in themselves. Words which will help change the course of our civilization from inside. That is one good reason why it was forbidden to utter one's "Magical Name" aloud, yet encouraged to sound it constantly in one's interior secret self. The point was to keep steadily and continually radiating one's fundamental change-frequency in the direction of Divinity. When this is activated, the rest will resolve into matters of arranging and channelling the resultant force.

One point has to be made entirely and absolutely clear. There must be nothing whatever of a coercive nature about the inner influence mediated from these higher levels towards our fellow mortals. That is to say, we should not deliberately impose our own purely personal ideas upon it in the sense of trying to compel others into compliance with our dictates. Any attempts of that kind would only distort and interfere with the influence, making it ineffective or misleading with regard to its original mission. A "Word" must never be deliberately *imposed* on anyone, but only made available and *offered*. It is then for all to accept, refuse or modify it as they will.

Human nature requires an awful lot of alteration, especially for the better. Every single contribution of adapted consciouness aimed in that general direction is of value. Magically made contributions are of special value, because they are constructed with the close co-operation of inner intelligences concerned with humanity. Not only that, but the various strains of our human race have their particular contacts of inner guardianship which offer the most direct and convenient means for making spiritual relationships. It is the unique responsibility of modern Western magi to seek and keep the closest contact possible with those special sources of cosmic co-operation.

Whether such magic is worked by ritualistic or other methods is beside the point. Ritualism is but a single branch on our mystical Tree of Inner Life. It is undoubtedly important, demanding valuable discipline, and certainly an essential factor of our Tradition. Yet it is purely supportive to our principle spiritual purpose. In the end, the entire meaning of magic within the

Western Tradition is *change*—change of conditions, states, circumstances, persons, places, and consciousness. Our magical legends and myths are tales of transformation. The most magical change of all times is that of a Sacred King from humanity to Divinity. Man into God is not only our ultimate magic, but also the highest heritage handed down to us in our days through our secret spiritual Tradition.

Therefore, even the least magical intention or activity worked within the West should be seen as a slight step in that Divine direction. Before contemplating any magical operation whatever, the motivating question should be asked: "What am I intending to change? Myself? Others? From what to what? Why?" and so forth. Only when clear ideas on those issues are obtained should any magical procedures be initiated. For example, prior to quite minor meditations it might be formulated: "I am trying to change my condition of consciousness from mundane objectivity to an inner awareness of such and such for the purpose of so and so." Once the change-motivation becomes plainly recognized, it will make a surprising difference. Unexpected channels open up in the mind, and go-aheads appear in otherwise dubious and difficult approaches.

Through the centuries, our Western Inner Tradition has accommodated itself to all sorts of changes in order to continue its message among us. Now it faces our most challenging change in history. Are we to remain on earth as a mass of manipulated mediocrities, or realize a relationship with each other as integrative individuals looking for higher life-levels? Which? Our entire Tradition belongs with the principles of Deliverance, Liberation, Emancipation, Self-government, in the sense of giving people full responsibility for their civil and cosmic behavior.

In the past, when the fundamentals of our Tradition were threatened by inimical invaders of our "spiritual space", our "inner aristocracy" led us toward liberation utilizing hidden reservoirs of faith in our own "right-rootedness". From those powerful points were sent out supplies and assistance of all kinds. As a rule, the humans concerned usually shook themselves sufficiently alert to push aside some immediate perils, turned torpidly away, and dozed off again until the next danger became too obvious to avoid. So we have more or less muddled from one crisis of consciousness to another through the ages.

Nothing could be more dangerous to those within the Western Tradition than blindly relying upon our "Inner Guardians" to avert all the evils we engender for ourselves in this world. If we sincerely want those evils abated we shall have to do that ourselves while we are incarnate, however much we need help from higher hands than ours. The magic which works best in this world has to be worked by and through those of this world. If humans are to be affected by magic, then human agencies must be used for that purpose one way or another. Our spiritual supporters may be able to push inner powers right up to our very gates, but if we really intend using these powers on our living levels here, we shall have to bring them through those portals ourselves and mediate them among fellow men and women. Otherwise we might as well abandon our Tradition altogether and let ourselves be overtaken by its opponents under conditions of their choice.

To be truly effective, modern magic must extend into every field of human experience. In science, for instance, it should emerge as some specialized part of the scientific scene. In religion, it could appear as a re-vitalizing influence connected with Christian or other systematic credo-concepts. In all cultural directions it has to make its mark unobtrusively yet acceptably to average Western awareness. It has already camouflaged itself under the general heading of "Parapsychology," which covers procedures previously only known and practiced by initiatory groups. Even the arcane activities of ritual magic itself are steadily classifying themselves as "psychodramatics". Not a single fundamental principle has been changed in the slightest, but by altering attitudes through changing concepts, magic is at last returning in the West to its primal position of importance in our living Tradition.

The obvious danger of this is if over-riding control of those currents should come into the wrong hands and be used for evil ends. Legends of the West are full of stories about past civilizations destroyed by and for that very reason. Atlantis, the antedeluvian world and Mu are just two examples. Whether factual or not, the warning is built into our Traditional tales, and is also staring us straight in the face as a present possibility.

When enough humans realize that setting their world right starts with setting themselves right, magic will work more wonders than anything else. Facilitating this process is un-doubtedly the most important function of future magical and occult movements within the Western Tradition. It may well be that technical terms and systems will change considerably to suit arising needs and circumstances, but underneath everything, linkages with our Traditional lines will continue. One notable advance will be the fade-out of old authoritarian associations in favor of self-selective circles of co-partners acting in mutually compensative harmony. Outgrown "grades" and antiquated "Titles", together with procedures now purposeless, will be superseded by improved techniques and customs more in keeping with modern capabilities. People will tend to find their rightful places for themselves within any human grouping rather than be pushed into positions by some "Supreme Council." Because of improving communications, more and more people who are conscious of Tradition will be drawn together. They can then make a magical choice of closer companionship for the sake of more highly specialized spiritual workings.

To take a couple of examples emerging in this century, we have the rather unusual upsurgence of interest in "leys", and reputed ground Zodiacs or other topographical designs in specific localities. The "magic" of these lies in their patterning associated with natural countryside and "native soil". One directs conscious-ness in straight lines like light, and the other in circles like currents of energy. Though their devotees may not be entirely aware of the fact, both these interests encourage the use and application of consciousness in concerted efforts according to inner specifications. Additionally, by inducing people to associate closely in mind and body with their own earthly outdoor environments through those particular patterns they can be brought into nearer contact with our Western inner intelligences using these natural media as channels of communication. Altogether it could be said that what seem like rather harmless and healthy hobbies are actually esoteric exercises of a "broad-band" type, aimed at conditioning modern consciousness along specific "folk-frequencies".

Maybe the same might be said for the practice of "saucer-spotting". Not many humans nowadays care to spend contempla-tive night-sessions on hill tops seeking spiritual contacts. Per-suade them there could be a million-to-one chance of glimpsing some inter-planetary vehicle and some will form their circles and concert their consciousness just as their ancestors did for somewhat different reasons. Few may spot anything like a spacecraft, but quite a number may benefit from inner influences concentrated on their little gatherings. Almost any interest which encourages people to focus attention while among quiet country conditions of their native land creates a spiritual situation suitable for contacts with agencies belonging with our Inner Tradition. Even bird-watching has such possibilities. Relate the common denominators of calm, attentive awareness, and suitable surroundings, and these will automatically produce a focal framework for inner communicative contacts.

Another sign in our times is the almost general acceptance of telepathy, or direct contacts of consciousness between beings through some unknown medium. Yet another connected concept is the possibility of telepathic communication with people living on other planets in different solar systems. As someone has said, the "spirit guides" of the last century have become the "spacemen" of this one. Looking back over our shoulders, we can see how our beliefs in supernatural entities, fairies, etc., descended to the spirits of departed relatives, and are now aimed at alternative life-forms existing in psychically connected physical galaxies. We alter our concepts of "other-life", but continue our fundamental feelings about them according to contemporary custom. Modern minds which firmly reject all ideas of archangels or divinities whatever, will cheerfully conceive notions of incredibly superior creatures to mankind, providing these are attached to some form of physical expression in remote corners of the Cosmos. Science-fiction writers have taken over from the old fairy-tale tellers, and no doubt in their turn will be superseded by some related style of romance. At the back of everything as usual, our Inner Tradition moves our shared subconsciousness steadily along towards the next step ahead.

Although our present epoch has not apparently produced any noteworthy movements to compare with Spiritualism, Hermeticism, and Theosophy of the last century, its mid-century miscalled "occult explosion" was indicative of a most significant spiritual fact. It marked a jumping off point for what has been called the "Alternative society." By contrast to the majority of money-minded consumer class people in our atomic age, an appreciable number of folk tended to disengage themselves from the competitive, compulsive, and computerized world of modernized man. Dissenters from "prosperity pressures" were quite willing to live amiably in conditions of relative poverty and material disadvantage, providing their independence of ideology was not seriously interfered with. For them, inner expansion of experience had become far more important than outer acquisition of position and property. In furtherance of that aim, they investigated everything available of an occult character whether connected with the Western Tradition or not. The total value of all that effort is more than difficult to even guess at.

We may deplore the horrors of drug abuse, disease, and all the unhappy issues arising from this painful rebirth of an "alternative society". It is easy to regret the commercial exploitation of the event with its junk journalism, hack-written rehashed literature, toyshop trash impedimenta, and the rest of the rubbish marketed for prodigious profits. We can criticize conduct, and say what we will about the stupidities and futilities associated with "subculturism" in the sixties, which may be true enough. Amid that miserable muddle was germinating a seed which could yet grow into a very surprising new branch of our Tradition. A forked branch, pointing to devaluation of materialistic standards on one hand, and sterling appreciation of spiritual standards on the other. What will happen within the West if we start breeding a strange new strain among us which resolutely refuses to conform with computer controlled frameworks of the future planned for us by an oligarchical ownership? Suppose people of this sort were indifferent to politicans of any party, had no interests in making money beyond basic necessities, were not impressed by social status, cared nothing for television, gambling, advertising, or much else that makes up the commercial pseudo-structure of our civilization. What happens if they firmly reject the modern Mammon archetype now officially appointed as our sociological savior, and offer allegiance to none but a Divinity reached in their own depths? The only prediction to be made regarding such a possibility is that it would prove highly unpopular with politicians, and absolutely anathema to the authorities.

Let us extrapolate this alternative society a bit further. Suppose it becomes a lot better than collections of drug sodden drop-outs and eccentrics. What if it should slowly be built up by evolved and capable young people with an extraordinary power of resistance to contemporary currents of cut-throat commercialism, pressure-politics, controls by criminal consortia, and other overwhelming wrongs ruining our world? Suppose again these folk have neither intentions nor interests of pouring all their energies into schemes for grabbing more money than others at the expense of their own inner integrity? Maybe they could be content with minimum living necessities in exchange for maximum time and opportunities of helping fellow humans find similar freedoms themselves. What if their chief concerns are far from profit-pursuits, but committed to causes of higher human aims like ecology, evolution, living relationships with beyond-body consciousness.

Thinking somewhat further ahead, what if it occurs to such young hopefuls that instead of opposing any Establishment openly, it would be more practical to infiltrate and alter things from the inside. Going further in still, suppose some of them find the secret of becoming born among the "circles of the elect", with sufficient "sense of mission" for accomplishing some specific life-aim in aid of less privileged people. Given enough effort along these inner lines, it could mean in the long run that control of human affairs in this world would change hands considerably for the better. Quite gently and genetically, the reins of government here might be transferred to more trustworthy fingers even before bodily birth. None need anticipate any spectacular victory of "virtue over vice" or remarkable predominance of pure philanthropy on these levels of life. Nevertheless, if the critical balance of inner powers affecting our outer existence can be focused in the right way it will definitely decide the difference between doom or deliverance in the course of our destiny.

Meanwhile, what would happen if the "alternatives" worked out a parallel scheme of economy among themselves, something that eventually made them minimally self-sufficient for goods and services on a profit-free plan? There is nothing impossible about this whatever. The Amish community in America has been doing it successfully for several generations. In wider terms, it would mean a sort of "society within society" so to speak. One section motivated by materialism alone, and the other based on a faith-formula. Average humanity might then measure itself against either example and decide which way to go, or try compromising with both.

We have seen too often the sad failures of human communities comprised from every class and creed on earth. Our whole world is one such communal disaster, yet by no means a complete disaster. It is still survivable and transmutable if its Traditions stay true to themselves and support each other for the mutual benefit of all mankind. Within a single lifespan, we have witnessed not only an atomic explosion but an ideological one as well. People can blow apart like plutonium, too. Now we have to put the pieces together again and make a better picture—if we can. Every artist involved has some kind of idea for improvements, and our magical artists are bound to advance their versions. these cannot possibly be worse than many past sights in this world, and could at least inspire us with a vision of how to overcome present obstacles obscuring a far finer future.

Finding some suitable niche to live in magically among modern society is mostly a matter of values. "Alternatives" might not offer many material advantages, but they could supply a wealth of human relationship and cultural company not easily found otherwise. Perhaps their greatest gift would be a deep love and concern for fellow creatures of every kind. Truly they could be called "natives" who would "alter" human nature for the better. Certainly not in any "do gooding" sense, or by inflicting the least of their ideas on anyone. They would merely be encouraging other entities to become what is willed within them by the Creative Spirit behind their conscousness. Maybe our "Alternatives" should be considered the resurgence of an almost extinct breed—compassionately understanding human beings, very willing to work on earth because they know a sense of kindred with Divine and closer connected Life means very much more than any wealth of this world.

If developments in this direction appear in the West, taking into account the initial impact of occult influences during the past mid-century period, we could indeed be coming to a turning point in our Tradition. In reality, it would be the first and oldest fundamental of the Tradition coming full circle on a higher level. Originally, Western individuants moved away from compulsive collectivity into alternative areas. Now we can no longer do this physically, we shall have to create an independent state of society for serving our needs until humanity as a whole reaches a more satisfactory spiritual condition of civilization than evidenced during our epoch.

So, though this century may not have produced anything very spectacular in the nature of new religions, Societies, Occult Orders, and Movements, it may certainly have commenced something more spiritually important to the West than all these— an awakened determination to look for links between Divinity and Humanity within ourselves. As Dion Fortune once termed it: "The Yoga of the West." Yog meaning yoke, in the sense of conjoining complements by a central principle of poise.

Our Traditional way of accomplishing this was and is to set up synthetic symbolic conditions wherein some semblance of an ideal life may be momentarily achieved. By periodic use of this facility, we project consciousness ever closer to that as a constant state. In old times initiates went off by themselves into forests or deserts until they "attained" an altered awareness within themselves. As civilization expanded outward they built Lodges and Temples wherein they might fulfil the spiritual side of themselves in safety for limited periods, the emerge to share socio-economic living with others on whom some of their spiritual influence might "rub off". Christian church-going was meant to be a common form of this practice.

This stems from the deep human need for intimacy with one's own identity in order to contact much higher levels of consciousness. It amounts to symbolizing a Nil-nucleus out of which energy is expected to emerge for specific ends. This accounts for the care with which truly Magical Temples are constructed and concealed. This applies to other types of private spaces as well. Every field employs them one way or another. The artist's studio is an example. The physicist's laboratory is another. So is an author's "den", or a priest's study, or a monk's cell. All are physical focal points dedicated to communion with specialized types of consciousness. All have the common factors of seclusion and security, or a semblance thereof. They could be broadly compared with womb-conditions of gestation.

Today, this issue is becoming a very serious problem on the Western Path. The layout of modern living is making it more and more difficult to achieve those essential occasions of contempla-

tive inner contacts. Noise, social pressures, employment environments, and all our civil circumstances come into the picture.
Somehow, there has to be an answer enabling our aspirant
esotericists to focus up their contacts right on the factory floor, as
it were. As yet, no-one seems to have produced an entirely
satisfactory solution, mainly because our consciousness is still
adapting to swifty altering situations and structures. Moreover,
the problem is likely to go on for a few generations yet.
Nevertheless it has to be tackled, and reasonable procedures
evolved which anyone of average abilities can understand and
apply under most conditions of modern life. This particular
problem is actually a fairly urgent one, since it affects a large
proportion of people who could make very useful contributions to
our Tradition if encouraged and enabled by the right examples
and precepts. Therefore all advanced initiates of the Western Way
and their inner contacts would do well to put this piece of work
into the "immediate" category of their programs.

In times to come, maybe not so very distantly, there will be a
much awakened awareness in the West about the importance of
this particular point. Noise will be abated to minimum, and
meditative facilities made much more widely available. Perhaps
the day could come when quite ordinary people would no more
purchase a new property without a special "contemplation
chamber" than they would buy houses now without bathrooms
and lavatories. It could become normal practice for workers to be
allowed standard periods every so often for meditative exercises.
We might even see "zoning" of population into quiet and noisy
areas, so that those who want racket and restlessness can have it
to heart's content providing they do not invade the places of
peace. We all have our ideas for future improvements, but what is
needed most are present practicalities. Answers to questions like:
"How am I to study and practice Western occultism while I have to
earn my living as a machine operator all day and share a small flat
with my family at night?"

In this century, the three main Western streams of "Poet,
Peasant, and People" are coalescing. Into what? Dare we hope into
"Perceptives," souls with an awakened spiritual awareness of their
own meaning among mankind? Those who sense beyond doubt
the truths behind our Tradition, and will dedicate their incarnations to seeking and upholding these fundamentals of a common

Life-faith? Souls with a stature capable of rising above differences of opinion, dogma, and every lesser division among human approaches to Divinity while working with conditions of consciousness conjoining them all as efforts in evolution. Ours is a broad Tradition with room for many specialized sections providing each is linked in its own fashion with our familial Lightway. For we are indeed a family on Inner levels of Life, related by a bond of blood which is none the less binding because it cannot be physically traced. We may symbolize this blood magically in the Mass, or see it metaphorically with our martyrs and massacred fellow men. However we represent it, our inner "belonging with the Blood" amounts to the "Grail Vision" where participants realized with full force their actual spiritual standing in the Presence of Perfection. Nothing bound them into closer company than that experience.

Every ex-Service person knows the instant sense of companionship springing up when two people previously unknown to each other discover they have shared some common episode of previous pressure. It may be anything from a barracks to a battle, but it always has to be whatever caused deep emotive reactions which have somehow altered the life-patterns of those reminiscing about them. Similar senses of solidarity can come from any set of circumstances. A school, workplace, wherever mutual endurance is involved. That is something like the feeling which should link the Western Traditionalists together in this world, except that we need not necessarily be physically aware of each other's proximity. What really matters is that we become conscious of our existence together as evolving individuals sharing the same Lifestream along a common Cosmic course. Our unity is not a matter of terrestrial geography but of sheer spiritual genetics and inherency. Whoever "belongs with the Blood" must learn how to recognize and respect it in others, however distant the relationship may be. Our survival as a species depends on that.

In the end, there is only one way of belonging with our Western Inner Tradition: live it constantly during embodiment and disembodiment. There is nothing to join like a cult or a club. The entrance is only to be found by individual souls within themselves, leading to a common consciousness illuminated by the same Light. To connect this with our objective living as human beings, we need only set up an appropriate symbolic framework and let the related inner forces focus through this accordingly. Otherwise they will remain unobtrusively at the back of our beings, working faithfully away as usual at the slow and thankless task of our spiritual supervision.

None need doubt for a single instant that there is an Inner Way of the West, though it can be very difficult to recognize and harder yet to follow. It is not for everyone—why should it be? There are Inner Ways to suit every sort of soul in existence, and this happens to be ours in particular. It matches our inner make-up and corresponds with the courses of consciousness we have been keeping through the centuries from birth to rebirth. Others are entitled to criticize or comment on it as they like. We that are of the Way ourselves are only obliged to try and leave every lifetime in a better condition than we came to it. By the time we are reborn within it, we should bring further contributions of consciousness to unfold along our lines of living. So the cycles ought to continue, as the Tradition builds bit by bit towards its ultimate Truth.

It is easy to follow the track of a Tradition by its outstanding events. It is equally easy to miss the fundamental importance of its almost unnoticable details distributed throughout the whole. People point to the peaks of mountains, but how often do they think of the single grains of matter constituting the entire heap? So with our Western Tradition. It is a conscious compendium of countless little lives each adding something of itself to the total we have arrived at now. Those are the tiny pieces that make it great. The particular pieces attracting attention merely mark out its mass. If any member of the Tradition were asked: "What have you given?" none could answer more than: "Myself" or less than "Loyalty", for that is the top and bottom of everything to do with it.

Surely this is worth much—to feel and know for certain in oneself that there really is a better kind of life to be reached and realized eventually. A state of being far beyond the sick and sorry condition of this man-mismanaged world. A Tradition to belong with so deeply and definitely as to say with complete sincerity: *"These are my people. They want me as I want them for what we are to one another. We are linked together by love and trust that none of us would willingly break. Though all of us are individuals, we live in and through each other. As my bodies die they will make more for me to reincarnate in if I have to. In or out of incarnation, I mean to follow this Way with my spiritual kinsfolk. Along my Path I expect every kind of human experience; joy, sorrow, pain, pleasure, all that ever happens to humans. Right through the middle of everything runs our Line of Light leading to ultimate Perfection and Peace. That is the inmost Truth of our Tradition, and if I can stay with it I shall become the Self I ought to be as an immortal entity of Living Energy. At last I have found the home where my heart is happy in the real meaning of the word. Here is where I belong by birthright, ancestry, nature, intention, and all that ever will be mine. In every life, THIS IS MY BODY I AM BOUND TO BY MY BLOOD. My Grail is gained. I and mine own are One forever."*

Whoever senses in themselves something of this sort has connected up consciously with their own Inner Tradition. All it needs is gentle awakening, like the Sleeping Princess, with a kiss of love as realisation begins to dawn that the Traditional Way of the West went away from this earth altogether. It went into the radiant glories of the sunset skies where lay the Land of the Blessed. None spoke of the beauties and wonders awaiting arrivals there, because those were more than mortals could comprehend. All anyone knew for certain was that if only we kept faithfully and patiently following our West-pointing Path, we should become part of such Perfection in the end.

SO MAY WE ALL
AMEN.